THE
HISTORY
OF
ISSUES

Terrorism

THE
HISTORY
OF
ISSUES

Terrorism

Michelle E. Houle, *Book Editor*

Bruce Glassman, *Vice President*
Bonnie Szumski, *Publisher*
Helen Cothran, *Managing Editor*

GREENHAVEN PRESS
An imprint of Thomson Gale, a part of The Thomson Corporation

THOMSON
————✳————™
GALE

Detroit • New York • San Francisco • San Diego • New Haven, Conn.
Waterville, Maine • London • Munich

THOMSON
GALE

LIBRARY OF CONGRESS CATALOGING-IN-PUBLICATION DATA

Terrorism / Michelle E. Houle, book editor.
    p. cm. — (The history of issues)
Includes bibliographical references and index.
ISBN 0-7377-1909-5 (lib. : alk. paper) — ISBN 0-7377-1910-9 (pbk. : alk. paper)
    1. Terrorism. 2. Terrorism—History. 3. Terrorism—Religious aspects. I. Houle, Michelle E. II. Series.
HV6431T4573 2005
303.6'25—dc22   2004049716

Printed in the United States of America

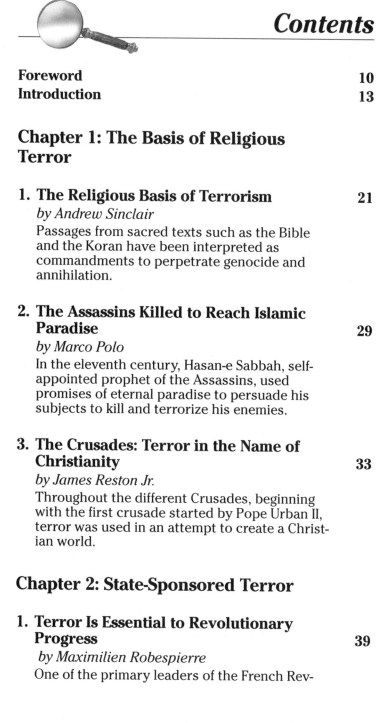

Contents

olution defended the use of terrorism to protect the new government. As a result, tens of
thousands perished in the Reign of Terror.

Chapter 3: Terror in the Name of National Liberation

Chapter 4: Terrorism and the United States

Foreword

In the 1940s, at the height of the Holocaust, Jews struggled to create a nation of their own in Palestine, a region of the Middle East that at the time was controlled by Britain. The British had placed limits on Jewish immigration to Palestine, hampering efforts to provide refuge to Jews fleeing the Holocaust. In response to this and other British policies, an underground Jewish resistance group called Irgun began carrying out terrorist attacks against British targets in Palestine, including immigration, intelligence, and police offices. Most famously, the group bombed the King David Hotel in Jerusalem, the site of a British military headquarters. Although the British were warned well in advance of the attack, they failed to evacuate the building. As a result, ninety-one people were killed (including fifteen Jews) and forty-five were injured.

Early in the twentieth century, Ireland, which had long been under British rule, was split into two countries. The south, populated mostly by Catholics, eventually achieved independence and became the Republic of Ireland. Northern Ireland, mostly Protestant, remained under British control. Catholics in both the north and south opposed British control of the north, and the Irish Republican Army (IRA) sought unification of Ireland as an independent nation. In 1969, the IRA split into two factions. A new radical wing, the Provisional IRA, was created and soon undertook numerous terrorist bombings and killings throughout Northern Ireland, the Republic of Ireland, and even in England. One of its most notorious attacks was the 1974 bombing of a Birmingham, England, bar that killed nineteen people.

In the mid-1990s, an Islamic terrorist group called al Qaeda began carrying out terrorist attacks against American targets overseas. In communications to the media, the organization listed several complaints against the United States. It generally opposed all U.S. involvement and presence in the Middle East. It particularly objected to the presence of U.S. troops in Saudi Arabia, which is the home of several Islamic holy sites. And it strongly condemned the United States for supporting the nation of Israel, which it claimed was an oppressor of Muslims. In 1998 al Qaeda's leaders issued a fatwa (a religious legal statement) calling for Muslims to kill Americans. Al Qaeda acted on this order many times—most memorably on September 11, 2001, when it attacked the World Trade Center and the Pentagon, killing nearly three thousand people.

These three groups—Irgun, the Provisional IRA, and al Qaeda—have achieved varied results. Irgun's terror campaign contributed to Britain's decision to pull out of Palestine and to support the creation of Israel in 1948. The Provisional IRA's tactics kept pressure on the British, but they also alienated many would-be supporters of independence for Northern Ireland. Al Qaeda's attacks provoked a strong U.S. military response but did not lessen America's involvement in the Middle East nor weaken its support of Israel. Despite these different results, the means and goals of these groups were similar. Although they emerged in different parts of the world during different eras and in support of different causes, all three had one thing in common: They all used clandestine violence to undermine a government they deemed oppressive or illegitimate.

The destruction of oppressive governments is not the only goal of terrorism. For example, terror is also used to minimize dissent in totalitarian regimes and to promote extreme ideologies. However, throughout history the motivations of terrorists have been remarkably similar, proving the old adage that "the more things change, the more they remain the same." Arguments for and against terrorism thus boil down to the same set of universal arguments regardless of the age: Some argue that terrorism is justified to change (or, in the case of state terror, to maintain) the prevailing political order; others respond that terrorism is inhumane and unacceptable under any circumstances. These basic views transcend time and place.

Similar fundamental arguments apply to other controversial social issues. For instance, arguments over the death penalty have always featured competing views of justice. Scholars cite biblical texts to claim that a person who takes a life must forfeit his or her life, while others cite religious doctrine to support their view that only God can take a human life. These arguments have remained essentially the same throughout the centuries. Likewise, the debate over euthanasia has persisted throughout the history of Western civilization. Supporters argue that it is compassionate to end the suffering of the dying by hastening their impending death; opponents insist that it is society's duty to make the dying as comfortable as possible as death takes its natural course.

Greenhaven Press's The History of Issues series illustrates this constancy of arguments surrounding major social issues. Each volume in the series focuses on one issue—including terrorism, the death penalty, and euthanasia—and examines how the debates have both evolved and remained essentially the same over the years. Primary documents such as newspaper articles, speeches, and government reports illuminate historical developments and offer perspectives from throughout history. Secondary sources provide overviews and commentaries from a more contemporary perspective. An introduction begins each anthology and supplies essential context and background. An annotated table of contents, chronology, and index allow for easy reference, and a bibliography and list of organizations to contact point to additional sources of information on the book's topic. With these features, The History of Issues series permits readers to glimpse both the historical and contemporary dimensions of humanity's most pressing and controversial social issues.

Introduction

Even in destruction, there's a right way and a wrong way—and there are limits.
　　　　　　　　　　—Albert Camus, *The Just Assassins*

Terrorism is the calculated use of violence, or the threat of violence, to intimidate, frighten, or coerce. Beyond those recurring elements, however, the complex concept of terrorism has no universally accepted or simple definition. Terrorism may be carried out, for example, by an individual, a group, or a government. Its motivation may be religious, political, or ideological. It is most closely associated with killing, maiming, kidnapping, hostage taking, and destruction of property, but cannot be limited to those acts.

It is a crime, but, as Rich Mkhondo of the Crimes of War Project explains, "Terrorism is more than simple violence which requires only two parties, an aggressor and a victim. Terrorism needs a third party, who might be intimidated by what happened to the victim."[1] The third party is usually an existing political institution, which terrorism aims to destabilize or overthrow.

Terrorism has been a constant feature of warfare throughout history, but it is not warfare because terrorism intentionally victimizes civilians and usually is not conducted by the armed forces of an established state. One way historians, theologians, and ethicists have attempted to differentiate terrorism from warfare, and to determine if terrorism is ever justified, is by subjecting a terrorist act or movement to a sort of test, to see if under examination it meets the moral standards by which Western civilization has judged the rightness of war for more than fifteen hundred years. This set of moral standards is known as just war theory.

Just War Theory

Though nonviolent resolution of disputes is a fundamental principle of social organization and religious teachings, most people have come to accept the idea that in a civilized society there are legitimate reasons to wage war and legitimate ways to wage it. Just war theory originated in the propositions of the first-century B.C. Roman orator and statesman Cicero, who sought to establish legal grounds for resolving disputes by armed conflict. Cicero proposed that only the Roman state could legitimately initiate war, and then only to recover lost property or rights. He maintained that deceptive military tactics such as ambushes could not be justified and that a victor was bound to show mercy to a defeated foe who had fought honorably.

The great Christian theologian and philosopher Augustine of Hippo expanded on Cicero's philosophy from a Christian perspective in the fifth century A.D. Augustine developed his argument on moral grounds: God, he wrote, had invested the state with certain rights to which individuals were not entitled, including the right to make war as long as the state acted with the intention to do good and avoid evil. St. Thomas Aquinas elaborated on Augustine's philosophy in the thirteenth century, emphasizing just cause and right intention. Over time this historical tradition split into two legal concepts, known by the Latin phrases *jus ad bellum* (laws to justify war) and *jus in bello* (laws for conduct during war). In the twentieth century international organizations such as the League of Nations and the United Nations promoted five main considerations as the basis of *jus ad bellum* arguments justifying war:

1. It must be conducted by legitimate civil authorities.
2. Its intention must be noble, such as ending suffering or oppression, and the good it is intended to achieve

must be proportional to the pain and damage it is likely to inflict.
3. It must be defensive, never aggressive.
4. It must only be undertaken as a last resort.
5. There must be a reasonable probability that it can accomplish its goal.

Generally, five principles guide the conduct of a just war (*jus in bello*):
1. Noncombatants, or civilians, must not be attacked.
2. Torture must never be used.
3. Prisoners must be treated humanely.
4. Means must be proportional to the actual threat presented by the enemy.
5. No acts of vengeance are permitted when the fighting is over.

Terrorism That Fails Just War Criteria

By these criteria, terrorist acts cannot be justified because they are committed either for illegitimate reasons or by illegitimate means. Terrorists violate not only national or international law but also the moral and ethical precepts by which just wars are waged. In short, terrorism provokes outrage because it breaks the rules of civilized society.

Historical examples abound of unjustifiable terrorism committed by recognized nation-states in wartime. During the long-running Jewish-Roman wars of antiquity, Roman emperors quashed opposition with terror tactics including torture and the abduction of political prisoners. Public beheadings during the eighteenth-century French Revolution came to symbolize the inhumanity of the Reign of Terror. Some argue that the devastation of civilian goods and property and the burning of Atlanta, Georgia, during Union general William T. Sherman's Civil War "march to the sea" crossed the line from military campaign to terrorism. And like many other captives throughout history, American prisoners of war were tortured by Communist North Vietnam during the Vietnam War.

The Nazi regime grossly violated just war theory. The Holocaust is one of history's most infamous examples of state-sponsored terrorism.

Nazi Germany under dictator Adolf Hitler is one of history's most notorious examples of state-sponsored terrorism carried to horrific extremes during wartime. The Nazi Party had consolidated its power through terror tactics such as brutal intimidation of civilians during the 1930s, justified by a thin veneer of legality. Hitler's reign of terror intensified during World War II, when he abandoned all adherence to just war principles and exterminated the Jews of Europe and other minority groups in the Holocaust. Hitler's Third Reich violated just war theory by its aggression and its institutionalization of torture and terror against civilian populations.

Most terrorist acts committed by nonstate actors also violate the criteria of just war theory. A clear example is Timothy McVeigh's bombing of the federal building in Oklahoma City in 1995. McVeigh justified his act as politically motivated retaliation for the U.S. government's role in the destruction of a Texas religious sect, and claimed his victims were guilty by association as federal employees. However, McVeigh had no legitimate civil authority; there was no likelihood that his act could achieve any just purpose; he had not first attempted alternative means of nonviolent protest, so his was not an act of last resort; and 19 of the 168 people he killed were children whose innocence was indisputable.

What is more controversial is the morality of terrorist acts by nonstate actors who, as analysts such as political scientist Andrew Valls suggest, can in principle satisfy the *jus ad bellum* criteria of just war theory.

Can Some Terrorist Acts Satisfy Just War Criteria?

Valls sparked heated debate with his 2000 essay "Can Terrorism Be Justified?" in which he points out a double standard in judging political violence: Political violence by states is permitted and sometimes even admired, while similar actions by nonstate actors are almost always universally condemned. Valls maintains that because in some cases nonstate actors *can* satisfy just war criteria, a single standard should apply: Terrorism by nonstate actors must be evaluated as morally right or wrong just as war by states is judged right or wrong, and the best test is just war theory.

For example, many political scientists argue that organizations such as the Palestine Liberation Organization (PLO) and the Irish Republican Army (IRA), though not recognized states, are legitimate representatives of religious and ethnic groups and thus have legitimate political authority. Satisfying this criterion is not enough, however. The PLO, though officially renouncing terrorism, has been linked to abhorrent terrorist activity such as random killing of civilians by suicide bombers, which violates other just war criteria and thus cannot be morally justified.

Unlike the Palestinian terrorist movement, the IRA is known to select targets to minimize civilian casualties, another criteria of just war theory. Most analysts agree, however, that IRA terrorism is nevertheless *not* justified because political solutions such as negotiation exist in lieu of violence, because IRA violence is unlikely to achieve the group's goal of uniting Northern Ireland with the Republic of Ireland, and because the suffering and evils of IRA terrorism outweigh the potential good unification would bring.

An often-cited example of justifiable terrorism is that of the African National Congress (ANC) against the apartheid regime of South Africa. Applying the *jus ad bellum* criteria of just war theory in this situation:

The ANC was the primary political party of South Africa's black majority, active from its inception in the late 1930s to 1961, when it was outlawed by the South African government, and from 1961 to 1990, when it operated as an underground militant resistance movement (legitimate civil authority). Its cause—the removal of an oppressive, racist government and the fight for equal rights for black South Africans—was applauded around the world (noble intention). The South African government supported apartheid with an apparatus of violent repression, including torture and murder (ANC reacted defensively). For decades, the ANC had advocated alternative methods of protest—marches and demonstrations, passive resistance, civil disobedience, negotiation—before resorting to terrorist tactics. At that point, the South African government had deprived blacks of the right to vote or strike and banned all opposition groups (last resort). Finally, the ANC campaign raised international awareness and sympathy, supported by trade embargoes that crippled the South African economy and pressured the government to dismantle apartheid (high probability of achieving its goal).

When *jus in bello* criteria are applied to ANC terrorism, the results are less clear-cut. The ANC bombing campaign primarily targeted military installations, members of the security forces, and official supporters of apartheid, not civilians. However, ANC militants also murdered white civilian South African farmers and tortured suspects under interrogation, which complicates the issue of justification even in this case.

Critics charge that evaluating terrorism on the same grounds as war between nations will give violence undeserved legitimacy and only encourage indiscriminate carnage. In making his case for assessing terrorism by just war criteria, however, Valls argues that terrorist acts cannot be delegitimized simply by applying the label:

> Most terrorist acts do not satisfy all of the criteria of just war theory and . . . many of them fall far short. In such cases we are well justified in condemning them. But the condemnation must follow, not precede, examination of the case and is not settled by calling the act terrorism and its perpetrators terrorists.[2]

Greenhaven's History of Issues *Terrorism* examines this complex subject to help readers define terrorism more clearly and join the debate over its possible justification more intelligently.

Notes

1. Rich Mkhondo, "Terrorism," Crimes of War Project, www.crimesof war.org/thebook/terrorism.html.
2. Andrew Valls, "Can Terrorism Be Justified?" in Andrew Valls, ed., *Ethics in International Affairs: Theories and Cases.* Lanham, MD: Rowman and Littlefield, p. 79.

THE
HISTORY
OF
ISSUES

CHAPTER 1

The Basis of Religious Terror

The Religious Basis of Terrorism

ANDREW SINCLAIR

In the following excerpt Andrew Sinclair argues that the three monotheistic religions have histories of terror, and their sacred texts have been used to justify terrorism. Ancient Israel was founded by means of genocide that was supposedly ordered by God. The Roman ruler Constantine used terror to eliminate subversive Christian sects. And Islamic terrorists have cited passages of the Koran to justify terrorist acts against nonbelievers. Sinclair is an author and historian who has written numerous books, including An Anatomy of Terror: A History of Terrorism, *from which this selection was excerpted.*

Of the three seminal religions of the Near East, Judaism and Christianity and Islam, the Jews founded Israel by a form of genocide. Moses said that the Lord had ordered the annihilation and subjugation of the original inhabitants of Canaan in a holy war. As Deuteronomy stated:

> When the Lord thy God shall bring thee into the land whither thou goest to possess it, and hath cast out many nations before thee, the Hittites, and the Girgashites, and the Amorites, and the Canaanites, and the Perizzites, and the Hivites, and the Jebusites, seven nations greater and mightier than thou;
>
> And when the Lord thy God shall deliver them before

thee; thou shalt smite them, and utterly destroy them; thou shalt make no covenant with them, nor shew mercy unto them . . .

For thou art an holy people unto the Lord thy God: the Lord thy God has chosen thee to be a special people unto Himself, above all people that are upon the face of the earth.

Joshua had particularly practised a policy of ethnic cleansing, as can be read in the biblical account of his reign, when he killed the population of Ai, men and women together to the number of 12,000, and burned the town. 'For Joshua drew not his hand back, wherewith he stretched out the spear, until he had utterly destroyed all the inhabitants of Ai . . . And Joshua burnt Ai, and made it an heap for ever, even a desolation unto this day.' He exterminated king after king and tribe after tribe, particularly in Hebron. 'And they took it, and smote it with the edge of the sword, and the king thereof, and all the cities thereof, and all the souls that were therein; he left none remaining'.

While Israel became more humane, with King David sparing the Jesubite citizens of his new Jerusalem, the Jewish faith always kept a militant streak. Yet revenge was taken on the Jews for their early annihilation of their enemies by King Tiglath-Pileser III of Assyria with his armies. The ten tribes of northern Judaea were conquered and enslaved and disappeared, never to be seen again except in the later fantasies of the British Israelites and American fundamentalist preachers.

The second disaster to hit Judaea was the razing of the Temple of Solomon and the deportation of the remaining two tribes of Israel to Babylon in 589 B.C. after the destruction of Jerusalem. They were allowed, however, to live in the first ghettos and practise their religion. Then the Medes and the Persians conquered the pagan city, and Cyrus allowed the Jews to return to their homeland and rebuild their Temple, which they did with a sword in one hand and a trowel in the other—an inspiration to the Freemasons to come.

In contrast to the aggressive Jewish faith, the paradox of Christianity was that Jesus had suffered from state terror. He was crucified as a sacrifice and intermediary between a cruel earth and a merciful heaven. Equally, the paradox of Islam was that the Prophet Muhammad was a general, who occupied pagan Mecca at the critical moment, when it might have fallen to a Christian Abyssinian army and gone to another faith.

The Cult of Christianity

Christianity began as a victim culture, suffering barbaric tortures. It was also organized as a secret society with cells, which later became chapels. It had code words such as the sign of the fish, the meaning of *Ichthys* in Greek letters, otherwise translated as an acronym for 'Jesus Christ, Son of God, Saviour'. The Roman governments thought of missionary Christianity as a heresy against the state religion of the Emperor, who was divine among other gods. The spread of the cult among the slave population encouraged revolts, such as that of Spartacus, who was also crucified with many of his followers.

Yet the subversive Christians seemed to be driven on by a martyr complex. Even if faced with torture or a rending by the beasts in the Circus Maximus, the Christians saw their self-sacrifice as an expiation on the way to heaven. Their suffering was their victory. They were soldiers of Christ, who had died so horribly in the holy war against the enemies of God.

As with Judaism and Islam, the great problem of any religion is when it passes from poverty to power. When the faithful are persuaded that they now rule through the leaders, a terrible revenge is exacted against those who disagree. Although old Rome fell to the barbarians, the Second Rome of Byzantium rose, later to be called Constantinople after its first Christian Emperor, Constantine. The heirs of the rebel apostles became the bishops and saints of the new power, which bridged Europe and Asia. Their worst barbarities were now inflicted on those who split hairs over the nature of the communion or the Trinity. Doctrinal differences became the material of massacre. When a revolutionary group takes over the state, it will persecute other rebel groups to preserve the fruits of the first revolution.

The Impact of Gnosis

During the spread of early Christianity, there was a multitude of interpretations of what the Torah and the Gospels meant. Many of these Gnostic texts were excluded from the final Bible. One of them, 'The Epistle to Rheginos', began by stating that there were some who wanted to learn much, but they were occupied with questions which had no answers. They had not stood within the Word or Logos of Truth. They sought their own solution, which could only come through Jesus Christ, who had denied death, which was the law of humankind. 'Those who are living shall die. How do they live in an illusion? The rich have become poor and the kings have been overthrown, everything has to change. The cosmos is an illusion.' All was a process, the transformation of things into newness, which would create a heaven from a corrupt society.

The authors of the Gnostic texts chose insight rather than the sermons of early Christian bishops to interpret the Gospels and reach revelation. On this count they were denounced in the late second century by St Irenaeus, the Bishop of Lyon, for 'inventing something new every day'. His chief target was Justin Martyr, who had been a Stoic and a Platonist before becoming a Christian philosopher. Justin praised the heresies of Simon Magus, the magician and enemy of St Paul, while Christ was treated as the Logos or Word, who mediated between the sinful earth and the light of paradise.

These inspirations were called Gnosis, which now came to mean a personal vision, a direct and individual perception of truth. The first appearance of Jesus to Mary Magdalene in the garden after His Crucifixion was interpreted in her apocryphal Gospel as no actual event or even a spiritual flash; she saw Him in her mind. This vision she reported to His disciples. They could now see the risen Christ as she had; any believer could see Him.

Of course, the direct approach to Christian revelation put in doubt all religious authority. Why listen to a bishop if an inner voice told you what Christ wanted you to do? In St Mark's Gospel, it was stated that Jesus had given the disciples the secret of the kingdom of God, while He spoke to the rest of the world in parables. While Saints Peter and Paul professed to pass on these secrets to the Churches later established in Rome and Byzantium, the Gnostic Gospels claimed that the living Jesus could at any time reveal His hidden mysteries to a woman who was not a disciple, to a Mary Magdalene, who represented the ancient female principle of generation, and the Sophia, the goddess of Wisdom. He should show Himself to the person who was fit to see and hear the divine message.

For the Gnostics, there were two distinct worlds, split by a war zone and a veil between heaven and earth. On the shining and dividing screen were the pictures of things, created by the Logos or Word and interpreted by Christ. Flaming walls separated wisdom from matter with angels as messengers across the horizon between sky and sea and land. The problem of evil allowed by a just God was solved, for life below was already hell.

Rebellion of Deviant Cults

While the Christians were still secret sects persecuted by the Roman Empire, such heresies could flourish among a larger heresy. Yet after Constantine established Christianity as the official faith, these subversive cults which declared that authority was evil had to be extirpated, although even the Byzantine Emperor would call his new basilica Sancta Sophia, not after any saint, but the wise goddess.

The more extreme of these sects were persecuted—the Orphites, who worshipped the wise Serpent; the Adamites, who held their ceremonies in the nude; and the Cainites, who cast aside all civil authority to venerate Cain carrying out the divine will by killing his brother Abel, as well as Judas, who was forced to denounce Jesus. As Irenaeus wrote of the teaching of the Gnostic 'Gospel of Judas', 'He alone was acquainted with the truth as no others were, and so accomplished the mystery of betrayal. By him all things, both earthly and heavenly, were thrown into dissolution.'

These doctrines of the personal revelation of a secret knowledge and of a continuing revolution were to be the motive forces of sacred terror movements within Christianity for two thousand years. Every state and each Church had to reject the rebellion of the cults. Once the Bible was defined within the limits of the Old and the New Testaments, allowing only the messianic and apocalyptical Book of Revelation inside its covers, all deviations from that holy norm might be pursued with fire and sword. The so-called heretics would be terrified into dissolution. Fear will drive men to any extreme, as [British author] George Bernard Shaw noted—as faith will, too.

Destruction of the Unbelievers

The Islamic creed was revealed to a tribal Arab war leader. In the seventh century, Muhammad was born in Mecca, then a pagan city with a cube, the Ka'aba, as a centre of worship. Inspired by the Angel Gabriel to form a new religion, Muhammad was ejected with his disciples to the nearby city of Medina. In his absence, Christian Abyssinian armies assaulted Mecca, but were turned back by disease. Muhammad began ambushing caravans and won a victory against superior forces at Badr, then he regained Mecca without a fight. As Christ had done with the moneychangers in the Temple at Jerusalem, the Prophet cast out all the idols from the Ka'aba except one, a black meteorite still kissed and revered in the hajj, the holy pilgrimage.

As did the Jews and the later Christians, Muhammad saw the reason for his victory in the hand of God or Allah. In the records of his sayings, the Qur'ān, he told his followers after Badr: 'It was not you but Allah who slew them. It was not you who smote them. Allah smote them so that He might richly reward His faithful. He hears and knows all. He will surely destroy the designs of the unbelievers.'

The inspiration of conquering Islam, which spread quickly over North Africa and the Near East after the death of the Prophet in 632, was his revelations, set down in the Qur'ān. As the ruler of Mecca, he had time to make laws and war and peace. He declared that he was the messenger of Allah, called to earth to form the missionary Umma, the global community of the Islamic faith. The divine purpose was to spread the Prophet's revelation to the far corners of the earth.

Like the Torah and the Bible, the Qur'ān was an ambiguous text, misused for political purposes by its various believers. The small groups of desert Bedouin who took over large areas in two continents had to practise tolerance towards other faiths, particularly Christians and Jews, in order to stay in power. Thus they preached texts from the Qur'ān such as: 'Truth is from Allah, therefore you shall not doubt. Every sect has a certain tract of heaven to which they turn themselves in prayer; but do you strive to run after good things.' And as a just and holy nation, the Arabs were commanded to pray towards the Ka'aba at Mecca. 'The direction of Allah is the true direction.'

Equally, other texts in the Qur'ān inspired a merciless war against all infidels.

> The Jews say, the Christians are grounded on nothing; and the Christians say, the Jews are grounded on nothing; yet they both read the scriptures. [*Indeed, the name of Jesus is mentioned ninety-three times in the Qur'ān.*] . . . But Allah shall judge between them on the day of the resurrection.

> Therefore the curse of Allah shall be upon the infidels.

For a vile price they have sold their souls, that they should not believe in that which Allah has sent down.

Fight for the religion of Allah against those who fight against you, but transgress not by attacking them first, for Allah loves not the transgressors. And kill them wherever you find them, and turn them from where they have dispossessed you. For temptation to idolatry is more grievous than slaughter.

Tragically, in modern times, Osama bin Laden convinced himself from the Qur'ān that the corruption of the United States and the continual conflicts over modern Israel were attacks on Islam, which justified his orders to kill the infidels, wherever his guerrilla pilots or suicide bombers found them. As a very wealthy man, he would certainly follow the Prophet's declaration: 'Contribute out of your substance toward the defence of the religion of Allah.' All sacred texts are misused, particularly by bellicose states or rebel terrorists, to justify the horrors which they perpetrate on civilian societies.

The Assassins Killed to Reach Islamic Paradise

MARCO POLO

In the late eleventh century an Iranian Isma'ili (member of a minority sect of Islam) named Hasan-e Sabbah put into action a battle plan to convert the world to his religion. Known by many names, including Aloadin and the Old Man of the Mountain, Hasan-e lived in the mountains south of the Caspian Sea in a seized fortress called Alamut. He cultivated a group of adolescent male followers by drugging them and taking them into a wholly constructed "paradise" designed to replicate Muslim descriptions of heaven. Once inside, the boys found an abundance of food, drink, and sexual favors. Hasan-e told his initiates, known as Assassins, or Ashishin, that that they must swear their allegiance to him. To secure a place for themselves in heaven they must obey all orders, including the murder of Hasan-e's Turkish and Persian enemies. The Assassins perfected the use of disguises and hit-and-run techniques in their terror campaigns. The cult of Hasan-e maintained wealth and power through its terrorist Assassins until 1255. Other Assassin cult "paradise" compounds were created in Damascus and Kurdistan. Hasan-e's successors continued the killings for hundreds of years. Hasan-e's politically and religiously trained Assassins and their use of sacred texts and guerrilla war tactics in many ways prefigured modern Islamic terrorist groups.

Marco Polo, *The Travels of Marco Polo*. London: John Murray, 1903.

Marco Polo related his knowledge of Alamut in his famous work The Travels, *excerpted here. Polo, who was born in Venice in 1254, toured extensively through China, India, Japan, and Persia until his death in 1323.*

Mulehet is a country in which the Old Man of the Mountain dwelt in former days; and the name means *"Place of the Aram."* I will tell you his whole history as related by Messer Marco Polo, who heard it from several natives of that region.

The Old Man was called in their language ALOADIN. He had caused a certain valley between two mountains to be enclosed, and had turned it into a garden, the largest and most beautiful that ever was seen, filled with every variety of fruit. In it were erected pavilions and palaces the most elegant that can be imagined, all covered with gilding and exquisite painting. And there were runnels too, flowing freely with wine and milk and honey and water; and numbers of ladies and of the most beautiful damsels in the world, who could play on all manner of instruments, and sung most sweetly, and danced in a manner that it was charming to behold. For the Old Man desired to make his people believe that this was actually Paradise. So he had fashioned it after the description that Mahommet gave of his Paradise, to wit, that it should be a beautiful garden running with conduits of wine and milk and honey and water, and full of lovely women for the delectation of all its inmates. And sure enough the Saracens of those parts believed that it *was* Paradise!

Now no man was allowed to enter the Garden save those whom he intended to be his ASHISHIN. There was a Fortress at the entrance to the Garden, strong enough to resist all the world, and there was no other way to get in. He kept at his Court a number of the youths of the country, from 12 to 20 years of age, such as had a taste for soldiering, and to these he used to tell tales about Paradise, just as Mahommet had been wont to do, and they believed in him just as the Saracens believe in Mahommet. Then he would introduce them into his garden, some four, or six, or ten at a time, having first made them drink a certain potion which cast them into a deep sleep, and then causing them to be lifted and carried in. So when they awoke, they found themselves in the Garden.

Ashishin Paradise

When therefore they awoke, and found themselves in a place so charming, they deemed that it was Paradise in very truth. And the ladies and damsels dallied with them to their hearts' content, so that they had what young men would have; and with their own good will they never would have quitted the place.

Now this Prince whom we call the Old One kept his Court in grand and noble style, and made those simple hill-folks about him believe firmly that he was a great Prophet. And when he wanted one of his *Ashishin* to send on any mission, he would cause that potion whereof I spoke to be given to one of the youths in the garden, and then had him carried into his Palace. So when the young man awoke, he found himself in the Castle, and no longer in that Paradise; whereat he was not over well pleased. He was then conducted to the Old Man's presence, and bowed before him with great veneration as believing himself to be in the presence of a true Prophet. The Prince would then ask whence he came, and he would reply that he came from Paradise! and that it was exactly such as Mahommet had described it in the Law. This of course gave the others who stood by, and who had not been admitted, the greatest desire to enter therein.

So when the Old Man would have any Prince slain, he would say to such a youth: "Go thou and slay So and So; and when thou returnest my Angels shall bear thee into Paradise. And shouldst thou die, natheless even so will I send my Angels to carry thee back into Paradise." So he caused them to believe; and thus there was no order of his that they would not affront any peril to execute, for the great desire they had to get back into that Paradise of his. And in this manner the Old One got his people to murder any one whom he desired to get rid of. Thus, too, the great dread that he inspired all Princes withal, made them become his tributaries in order that he might abide at peace and amity with them.

I should also tell you that the Old Man had certain others under him, who copied his proceedings and acted exactly in the same manner. One of these was sent into the territory of Damascus, and the other into Curdistan.

Now it came to pass, in the year of Christ's Incarnation, 1252, that Alalü, Lord of the Tartars of the Levant, heard tell of these great crimes of the Old Man, and resolved to make an end of him. So he took and sent one of his Barons with a great Army to that Castle, and they besieged it for three years, but they could not take it, so strong was it. And indeed if they had had food within it never would have been taken. But after being besieged those three years they ran short of victual, and were taken. The Old Man was put to death with all his men [and the Castle with its Garden of Paradise was levelled with the ground]. And since that time he has had no successor; and there was an end to all his villainies.

The Crusades: Terror in the Name of Christianity

JAMES RESTON JR.

In a speech delivered on November 17, 1095, Pope Urban II called for the liberation of Christian holy lands, including Jerusalem, from the Muslim Turks. Over a hundred thousand armed men and women responded to the papal charge and battled ferociously for the next six years. This marked the first of what would be five major bloody crusades over two hundred years against the "infidels." An equally important goal to the conquest of Christian holy lands was the ideological expansion of Christianity through religious conversion. Richard the Lionheart, British leader of the Third Crusade, directed his forces to convert or murder innumerable Muslims. Under the leadership of their revered leader Saladin, the Muslim people fought valiantly against the Christian terrorists. Saladin, a brilliant strategist and tactician, is still revered today in many parts of the world as a man who fought against the perpetrators of a Muslim holocaust.

Author James Reston Jr. is a journalist and documentary screenwriter. In the following excerpt he uses examples from the Third Crusade to argue that repercussions from the terror and extreme violence perpetrated by crusaders continues to resonate dramatically in modern-day politics and the Arab world.

James Reston Jr., *Warriors of God*. New York: Doubleday, 2001. Copyright © 2001 by James Reston Jr. Reproduced by permission of the publisher.

The crusader "movement," as it is sometimes called, stretched over a period of two hundred years, unleashing a frenzy of hate and violence unprecedented before the advent of the technological age and the scourge of Hitler. The madness was initiated in the name of religion by a Pope of the Christian Church, Urban II, in 1095 as a measure to redirect the energies of warring European barons from their bloody, local disputes into a "noble" quest to reclaim the Holy Land from the "infidel." Once unleashed, the passion could not be controlled. The violence began with the massacre of Jews, proceeded to the wholesale slaughter of Muslims in their native land, sapped the wealth of Europe, and ended with an almost unimaginable death toll on all sides. Bernard of Clairvaux, the great propagandist of the Second Crusade, would lament that he left only one man in Europe to comfort every seven widows.

There were five major crusades (and a handful of minor eruptions bred of the same instinct). Only the First Crusade was "successful," in the sense that it managed to capture Jerusalem and in the process make the streets of the Old City run ankle deep with Muslim and Jewish blood. All the others were failures. Three of the five got close to the object of the enterprise, the Holy City. Only because of the disunity of the Arab world did the First Crusade succeed in capturing Jerusalem. Precisely because of the unification of Egypt and Syria into a united Arab empire, the Third Crusade failed to capture it. In the Fifth Crusade, Frederick II of Germany negotiated his way into the Holy City, only to leave Palestine weeks later, pelted with garbage by his own people.

The Third Crusade, spanning the years 1187–92, is the most interesting of them all. It was the largest military endeavor of the Middle Ages and most important, it brought two of the most remarkable and fascinating figures of the last millennium into conflict: Saladin, the Sultan of Egypt, Syria, Arabia, and Mesopotamia; and Richard I, King of England, known as the Lionheart.

That conflict of giants in a grand holy tournament still

resounds in the modern history and modern politics of the present-day Middle East. Indeed, its resonance is even broader: with conflicts between Christians and Muslims wherever they may exist in the world, from Bosnia to Kosovo to Chechnya to Lebanon to Malaysia to Indonesia.

Saladin the Hero

Until this day Saladin remains a preeminent hero of the Islamic world. It was he who united the Arabs, who defeated the Crusaders in epic battles, who recaptured Jerusalem, and who threw the European invaders out of Arab lands. In the seemingly endless struggle of modern-day Arabs to reassert the essentially Arab nature of Palestine, Saladin lives, vibrantly, as a symbol of hope and as the stuff of myth. In Damascus or Cairo, Amman or East Jerusalem, one can easily fall into lengthy conversations about Saladin, for these ancient memories are central to the Arab sensibility and to their ideology of liberation. On the bars of the small, dimly lit cell in the Old City of Jerusalem where Saladin lived humbly after his grand conquests is the inscription, "Allah, Muhammad, Saladin." God, prophet, liberator. Such is Saladin's relation to the Muslim God.

The Arab world, it seems, is forever waiting for another Saladin. At Friday prayer, from Aleppo to Cairo to Baghdad, it is not unusual to hear the plea for one like him to come and liberate Jerusalem. His total victory over the Crusaders at the Battle of Hattin is held up today as the everlasting symbol of Arab triumph over Western interference. . . .

But it is not only for his military prowess that Saladin is venerated. He is also remembered for his humility, his compassion, his mysticism, his piety, and his restraint.

Richard the Lionheart: Warrior

The legacy of Richard I of England is no less vibrant but somewhat different in nature. He is one of the most romantic figures of all of English history. In lore that has been embellished over the centuries and read to schoolboys at bedtime, Richard has become the very epitome of chivalry, the knight fighting bravely for his kingdom, his church, and his lady with ax, shield, and horse. . . .

That in actual history, Richard Coeur de Lion did not quite measure up to the standards of his own legend does not dull his allure. He was a brilliant military mind and a fearsome general who understood the strategy and tactics of large forces far ahead of his time, just as in single combat he was unrivaled in bravery ahd recklessness. His enterprise, no matter what its final outcome, was incredible. And his return from the Holy Land and capture in Austria has the Homeric flavor of Odysseus. Richard is remembered for his bravado and cunning—and his extravagance. He is not remembered for his compassion, his tact, or his restraint. . . .

Modern Day Repercussions

The symbolism of the Third Crusade hovers over the modern history and modern politics of the Middle East. On December 11, 1917, when General Edmund Allenby walked through Jaffa Gate to accept the surrender of the Turks after four hundred years of rule, the press made much about the consummation of Europe's last crusade. In July 1920, when the French general Henri Gouraud took charge of Damascus, he strode to Saladin's tomb next to the Grand Mosque and exclaimed, to the everlasting disgust of modern Arabs, "Saladin, we have returned. My presence here consecrates the victory of the Cross over the Crescent.". . .

In Arabic literature today the Jews are seen as the modern crusaders, essentially European peoples who have invaded and occupied the Arab homeland. Just as a handful of crusaders controlled the Arab masses with their network of daunting fortresses and tight urban communities, so today, say Arab intellectuals, Israel controls the Arab majority with its American-backed military might and its fortified, barbed-wire-encircled hilltop settlements. It is an article of faith on the Arab side that through the slow and mysterious but inevitable forces of history, the Israelis, like the Crusaders, will eventually be forced out of Palestine. . . .

The Third Crusade was Holy War at its most virulent. Inevitably there was much about it that was unholy, indeed, sacrilegious: the pogroms of Jews, the lust for booty, the effusions of greed, the fighting and killing for their own sake—all in the name of piety. Here Holy War was in its infancy but practiced at the height of its ferocity. In the first instance it was a Christian Holy War that was met in response and in reaction by the Muslim concept of jihad. Jihad is, by definition, a defensive concept, conditioned upon the provocation of an unbelieving aggressor. In the Koran the believer is called upon "to fight in the way of God with those who fight with you . . . but aggress not: God loves not the aggressors" (2:190). From this holy and defensive fighting, great heavenly rewards will flow.

And so it is an irony of history that today, the word "jihad" strikes fear in the hearts of many Westerners and Western governments who associate it with terrorism and Islamic fanaticism. But there is nothing in Islamic history that rivals the terror of the Crusades or the Christian fanaticism of the twelfth century.

In the spring of 2000 the Crusades were back in the news. On the Sunday before his historic pilgrimage to the Holy Land, Pope John Paul II issued a sweeping apology for all the sins committed by the Roman Church in the name of religion over the past two thousand years. Called "Memory and Reconciliation," and following the 1992 apology for the treatment of Galileo, the proclamation was yet another act of digesting the dark episodes of church history at the millennium as part of a process the Holy See has called "historical purification." In the litany of atrocities against Jews, Muslims, women, and ethnic groups, the Crusades were specifically mentioned.

For the Muslim population in the Middle East, the papal pronouncement was cause for celebration. In the matter of religious apologies, the Crusades, at last, had received equal billing with the Holocaust.

THE
HISTORY
OF
ISSUES

CHAPTER 2

State-Sponsored Terror

Terror Is Essential to Revolutionary Progress

MAXIMILIEN ROBESPIERRE

Maximilien Robespierre, born in 1758, rose to power in the ruling body of revolutionary France known as the National Assembly. While head of the twelve-member Committee of Public Safety, which was created by the assembly to run the country, Robespierre called for the suppression of external and internal threats to the new government. He instituted a campaign known as the Reign of Terror, which resulted in the deaths of thousands of suspected opponents.

In this speech delivered on February 5, 1794, Robespierre argues that terrorism is a powerful leadership tool and a necessary weapon against the enemies of democracy who he claims threaten the revolutionary government. Robespierre was executed by guillotine in July 1794 after a botched suicide attempt.

To found and consolidate democracy, to achieve the peaceable reign of the constitutional laws, we must end the war of liberty against tyranny and pass safely across the storms of the revolution: such is the aim of the revolutionary system that you have enacted. Your conduct, then, ought also to be regulated by the stormy circumstances in which the republic is placed; and the plan of your administration must result from the spirit of the revolutionary

---

Maximilien Robespierre, speech on the justification of the use of terror, February 5, 1794.

government combined with the general principles of democracy.

Now, what is the fundamental principle of the democratic or popular government—that is, the essential spring which makes it move? It is virtue; I am speaking of the public virtue which effected so many prodigies in Greece and Rome and which ought to produce much more surprising ones in republican France; of that virtue which is nothing other than the love of country and of its laws.

But as the essence of the republic or of democracy is equality, it follows that the love of country necessarily includes the love of equality.

It is also true that this sublime sentiment assumes a preference for the public interest over every particular interest; hence the love of country presupposes or produces all the virtues: for what are they other than that spiritual strength which renders one capable of those sacrifices? And how could the slave of avarice or ambition, for example, sacrifice his idol to his country? Not only is virtue the soul of democracy; it can exist only in that government. . . .

Breaking Chains of Despotism

Republican virtue can be considered in relation to the people and in relation to the government; it is necessary in both. When only the government lacks virtue, there remains a resource in the people's virtue; but when the people itself is corrupted, liberty is already lost. Fortunately virtue is natural to the people, notwithstanding aristocratic prejudices. A nation is truly corrupted when, having by degrees lost its character and its liberty, it passes from democracy to aristocracy or to monarchy; that is the decrepitude and death of the body politic. . . . But when, by prodigious efforts of courage and reason, a people breaks the chains of despotism to make them into trophies of liberty; when by the force of its moral temperament it comes, as it were, out of the arms of the death, to recapture all the vigor of youth; when by turns it is sensitive and proud, intrepid and docile, and can be stopped neither by impregnable ramparts nor by the innumerable armies of the tyrants armed against it, but stops of itself upon confronting the law's image; then if it does not climb rapidly to the summit of its destinies, this can only be the fault of those who govern it. . . .

From all this let us deduce a great truth: the characteristic of popular government is confidence in the people and severity towards itself.

The whole development of our theory would end here if you had only to pilot the vessel of the Republic through calm waters; but the tempest roars, and the revolution imposes on you another task.

Virtue and Terror

This great purity of the French revolution's basis, the very sublimity of its objective, is precisely what causes both our strength and our weakness. Our strength, because it gives to us truth's ascendancy over imposture, and the rights of the public interest over private interests; our weakness, because it rallies all vicious men against us, all those who in their hearts contemplated despoiling the people and all those who intend to let it be despoiled with impunity, both those who have rejected freedom as a personal calamity and those who have embraced the revolution as a career and the Republic as prey. Hence the defection of so many ambitious or greedy men who since the point of departure have abandoned us along the way because they did not begin the journey with the same destination in view. The two opposing spirits that have been represented in a struggle to rule nature might be said to be fighting in this great period of human history to fix irrevocably the world's destinies, and France is the scene of this fearful combat. Without, all the tyrants encircle you; within, all tyranny's friends conspire; they will conspire until hope is wrested from crime. We must smother the internal and external enemies of the Republic or perish with it; now in this situation, the first maxim of your policy ought to be to lead the people by reason and the people's enemies by terror.

If the spring of popular government in time of peace is virtue, the springs of popular government in revolution are at once *virtue and terror:* virtue, without which terror is fatal; terror, without which virtue is powerless. Terror is nothing other than justice, prompt, severe, inflexible; it is therefore an emanation of virtue; it is not so much a special principle as it is a consequence of the general principle of democracy applied to our country's most urgent needs.

It has been said that terror is the principle of despotic government. Does your government therefore resemble despotism? Yes, as the sword that gleams in the hands of the heroes of liberty resembles that with which the henchmen of tyranny are armed. Let the despot govern by terror his brutalized subjects; he is right, as a despot. Subdue by terror the enemies of liberty, and you will be right, as founders of the Republic. The government of the revolution is liberty's despotism against tyranny. Is force made only to protect crime? And is the thunderbolt not destined to strike the heads of the proud? . . .

Indulgence for the royalists, cry certain men, mercy for the villains! No! mercy for the innocent, mercy for the weak, mercy for the unfortunate, mercy for humanity.

Society owes protection only to peaceable citizens; the only citizens in the Republic are the republicans. For it, the royalists, the conspirators are only strangers or, rather, enemies. This terrible war waged by liberty against tyranny—is it not indivisible? Are the enemies within not the allies of the enemies without? The assassins who tear our country apart, the intriguers who buy the consciences that hold the people's mandate; the traitors who sell them; the mercenary pamphleteers hired to dishonor the people's cause, to kill public virtue, to stir up the fire of civil discord, and to prepare political counterrevolution by moral counterrevolution—are all those men less guilty or less dangerous than the tyrants whom they serve?

Terrorism Against the Jews in Warsaw

SS OFFICER STROOP

During World War II the Nazi regime maintained a ghetto for Jews in German-occupied Warsaw, Poland. What follows are the reports of an SS officer named Stroop who commanded an operation between April 20 and April 25, 1943, that aimed to "clean out" any resistance to German domination. These reports provide a chilling illustration of state terrorism in action.

My intention is first to comb out completely the remainder of the Ghetto and then to clean out in the same manner the socalled uninhabited Ghetto, which so far has not been released. It had been ascertained in the meantime that the latter part of the Ghetto contains at least 10 to 12 dug-outs, some of which are even in armament factories. The whole operation is made more difficult because there are still factories in the Ghetto which must be protected against bombardment and fire, because they contain machines and tools.

A further report will follow tonight.

The SS and Police Fuehrer in the District of Warsaw. [signed] Stroop

SS-Brigadefuehrer and Majorgeneral of Police.

20 April 1943

The resistance centers ascertained with the uninhabited but not yet released part of the Ghetto were crushed by a battle group of the Wehrmacht-Engineers and flame throw-

---

SS Officer Stroop, "Message from the SS and Police Fuehrer in the District of Warsaw," April 20–25, 1943.

ers. The Wehrmacht had one wounded in this operation, shot through the lungs. Nine raiding parties broke through as far as the northern limit of the Ghetto. 9 dug-outs were found, their inmates crushed when they resisted, and the dug-outs blown up. What losses the enemy suffered cannot be ascertained accurately. Altogether the 9 raiding parties caught 505 Jews today; those among them who are able-bodied were kept ready for transport to Poniatowo. At about 1500 hrs. I managed to arrange that the block of buildings occupied by the Army Accommodation Office said to be occupied by 4,000 Jews is to be evacuated at once. The German manager was asked to call upon the Jewish workers to leave the block voluntarily. Only 28 Jews obeyed this order. Thereupon I resolved either to evacuate the block by force or to blow it up. The A.A. Artillery-3 2-cm. guns used for this operation had two men killed. The 10-cm howitzer, which also was used, expelled the gangs from their strong fortifications and also inflicted losses on them, as far as we were able to ascertain. This action had to be broken off owing to the fall of darkness. On 21 April 1943 we shall attack this resistance center again, as far as possible it will remain blocked off during the night.

"Cleaning" by Force

In today's action we caught, apart from the Jews reported above, considerable stores of incendiary bottles, hand grenades, ammunition, military tunics, and equipment. *Losses:*

2 dead (Wehrmacht) 7 wounded (6 Waffen SS, 1 Trawniki-man)

In one case the bandits had laid pressure mines. I have succeeded in causing the firms W.C. Toebens, Schultz and Co., and Hoffman to be ready for evacuation with their entire personnel on 21 April 1943 at 0600 hrs. In this way, I hope to get the way free at last for cleaning out the Ghetto. The Trustees Toebens has pledged himself to induce the Jews, numbering about 4,000 to 5,000, to follow him voluntarily to the assembling point for being resettled. In case this has as little success as was attained in the case of the Army Accommodation Office, I am going to clean out this part of the Ghetto as well by force. . . .

22 April 1943

One raiding party was dispatched to invade once more the block of buildings which for the greater part had burned out or was still aflame, in order to catch those Jews who were still inside. When shooting again started from one block against the men of the Waffen-SS, this block also was set on fire, with the result that a considerable number of bandits were scared from their hideouts and shot while trying to escape. Apart for those, we caught about 180 Jews in the yards of the buildings. The main body of our units continued the cleansing action from the line where we terminated this action yesterday. This operation is still in progress. As on the preceding days local resistance was broken and the dug-outs we discovered were blown up. Unfortunately there is no way of preventing part of the Jews and bandits from taking refuge in the sewers below the Ghetto, where we can hardly catch them since they have stopped the flooding. The city administration is not in a position to frustrate this nuisance. Neither did the use of smoke candles or the introduction of creosote into the water have the desired result. Cooperation with the Wehrmacht splendid. . . .

22 April 1943

When the special raiding party searched the remainder of the blocks as already reported, they met with resistance at some places; they had the following success: 1,100 Jews caught for evacuation, 203 bandits and Jews killed, 15 dugouts blown up. They captured 80 incendiary bottles and other booty. Units at my disposal: as reported by teletype message on 20 April 1943. Journal No. 516/43 secret.

Our losses: SS-Untersturmfuehrer Dehmke (dead); enemy hit a hand grenade which he carried. (SS-Cav. Res. Batl.)

1 Sergeant of Police (shot through the lungs)

When the Engineers blew up the dug-outs, a considerable number of Jews and bandits were buried under the ruins. In a number of cases it was found necessary to start fires in order to smoke the gangs out.

I must add that since yesterday some of the units have been shot at time and again from outside the Ghetto, that is, from the Aryan part of Warsaw. Raiding parties at once entered the area in question and in one case succeeded in capturing 35 Polish bandits, Communists, who were liquidated at once. Today it happened repeatedly when we found it necessary to execute some bandits, that they collapsed shouting "Long live Poland," "Long live Moscow.". . .

23 April 1943

The whole of the former Ghetto had been divided for the purposes of today's combing-out operations into 24 districts. One reinforced searching party was detailed to each district with special orders. These assignments had to be carried out by 1600 hours. Result of this action: 600 Jews and bandits ferreted out and captured, about 200 Jews and bandits killed, 48 dug-outs, some of them of a quite elaborate character, blown up. We captured—apart from valuables and money—some gas masks.

The units had been informed that we intended to terminate the operation today. In the morning the Jews had already become aware of this instruction. This is why a renewed search by the searching parties was undertaken after an interval of 1 to 1½ hours. The result was, as always, that again Jews and bandits were discovered to be in various blocks. From one block shots were even fired against the cordoning units. An attack by a special battle group was ordered and in order to smoke the bandits out, every building was now set on fire. The Jews and bandits held out, every building was now set on fire. The Jews and bandits held their fire up to the last moment and then concerted their fire against the units. They even used carbines. A number of bandits who were shooting from balconies were hit by our men and crashed down.

Furthermore, today we discovered a place said to have

been the headquarters of the "PPR"; we found it unoccupied and destroyed it. . . .

I found the worst of the terrorists and activists, who so far had always found ways and means to dodge every searching or evacuation action.

A racial German reported that again some Jews had escaped through the sewers into the Aryan part of the city. We learned from a traitor that there were some Jews in a certain house. A special motorized raiding party invaded the building and caught 3 Jews, 2 of them females. During this operation their motor-car was pelted with one incendiary bottle and one explosive; 2 policemen were wounded.

The whole operation is rendered more difficult by the cunning way in which the Jews and bandits act; for instance, we discover that the hearses which were used to collect the corpses lying around at the same time bring living Jews to the Jewish cemetery, and thus they are enabled

SS guards round up Jews for deportation to concentration camps during the Warsaw Ghetto uprising.

to escape from the Ghetto. Now this way of escape also is barred by continuous control of the hearses.

At the termination of today's operation about 2200 hours, we discovered that again about 30 bandits had passed into a so-called armaments factory, where they had found refuge. Since the forces are storing goods of great value in this enterprise, this factory was requested to evacuate the building by noon on 24 April; this will enable us to cleanse that labyrinth of a building tomorrow.

Today 3,500 Jews were caught who are to be evacuated from the factories. A total of 19,450 Jews have been caught for resettlement or already evacuated up to today. Of these about 2,500 Jews are still to be loaded. The next train will start on 24 April 1943. Strength as of 22 April 1943, without 150 Trawniki men; these have already been put at the disposal of the Eastern Command as reinforcement for another assignment.

Our losses:

2 Police corporals ("SB") wounded 1 Trawniki man wounded.

The operation will be continued on 24 April 1943, 1000 hours. This hour was chosen so that Jews who may still be in the Ghetto will believe that the operation was actually terminated today. . . .

24 April 1943

Contrary to the preceding days, the 24 searching parties which had again been formed did not start at one end of the Ghetto, but proceeded from all sides at the same time. Apparently the Jews still in the Ghetto were deceived by the fact that the operation did not start until 1000 hours into believing that the action really had been terminated yesterday. The search action, therefore, had especially satisfactory results today. This success is furthermore due to the fact that the noncommissioned officers and men have meanwhile become accustomed to the cunning fighting, methods and tricks used by the Jews and bandits and that they have acquired great skill in tracking down the dug-outs which are found in such great number. The raiding parties having returned, we set about to clean a certain block of buildings, [situated in the] northeastern part of the former Ghetto. In this labyrinth of buildings there was a so-called armaments firm which reportedly had goods worth millions for manufacture and storage. I had notified the Wehrmacht of my intentions on 23 April 1943 about 2100 hours, and had requested them to remove their goods by 1200 hours. Since the Wehrmacht did not start this evacuation until 1000 hours I felt obliged to extend the term until 1800 hours. At 1815 hours a search party entered the premises, the building having been cordoned off, and found that a great number of Jews were within the building. Since some of these Jews resisted, I ordered the building to be set on fire. Not until all the buildings along the street and the back premises on either side were well aflame did the Jews, some of them on fire, emerge from these blocks, some of them endeavored to save their life by jumping into the street from windows and balconies, after having thrown down beds, blankets, and the like. Over and over again we observed that Jews and bandits, despite the danger of being burned alive, preferred to return into the flames rather than risk being caught by us. Over and over again the Jews kept up their firing almost to the end of the action; thus the engineers had to be protected by a machine gun when toward nightfall they had to enter forcibly a concrete building which had been very strongly fortified. Termination of today's operation; on 25 April 1943 at 0145 hours. 1,660 Jews were caught for evacuation, pulled out of dug-outs, about 330 shot. Innumerable Jews Swede destroyed by the flames or perished when the dugouts were blown up. 26 dug-outs were blown up and an amount of paper money, especially dollars was captured; this money has not yet been counted.

Our forces; as on the preceding day, minus 50 men of the Waffen-SS.

Our losses: 2 SS men and 1 Trawniki man wounded.

Altogether there have now been caught in this action 25,500 Jews who lived in the former Ghetto. Since there are only vague estimates available of the actual number of inhabitants I assume that now only very small numbers of Jews and bandits still remain within the Ghetto.

Operation will be continued on 25 April 1943, 1300 hours.

I beg to acknowledge receipt of teletype messages Nos. 1222 and 1223 of 24 April 1943. As far as can be predicted, the present large-scale operation will last until Easter Monday inclusive.

Today large posters were affixed to the walls surrounding the Ghetto, announcing that everybody who enters the former Ghetto without being able to prove his identity will be shot. . . .

25 April 1943

For today 7 search parties were formed, strength 1/70 each, each allotted to a certain block of buildings.

Their order was: "Every building is to be combed out once more; dug-outs have to be discovered and blown up, and the Jews have to be caught. If any resistance is encountered or if dug-outs cannot be reached, the buildings are to be burnt down." Apart from the operations undertaken by these 7 search parties, a special operation was undertaken against a center of bandits, situated outside the wall surrounding the former Ghetto and inhabited exclusively by Poles.

Today's operations of the search parties ended almost everywhere in the starting of enormous conflagrations. In this manner the Jews were forced to leave their hideouts and refuges. A total of 1,960 Jews were caught alive. The Jews informed us that among them were certain parachutists who were dropped here and bandits who had been equipped with arms from some unknown source. 274 Jews were killed. As in the preceding days, uncounted Jews were buried in blown up dug-outs and, as can be observed time and again, burned with this bag of Jews today. We have, in my opinion, caught a very considerable part of the bandits and lowest elements of the Ghetto. Intervening darkness prevented immediate liquidation. I am going to try to obtain a train for T II tomorrow. Otherwise liquidation will be carried out tomorrow. Today also, some armed resistance was encountered; in a dug-out three pistols and some explosives were captured. Furthermore, considerable amounts of paper money, foreign currency, gold coins, and jewelry were seized today.

The Jews still have considerable property. While last night a glare of fire could be seen above the former Ghetto, today one can observe a giant sea of flames. Since we continue to discover great numbers of Jews whenever we search and comb out, the operation will be continued on 26 April 1943. Start: 1000 hours.

Including today, a total of 27,464 Jews of the former Warsaw Ghetto, have been captured. . . .

26 April 1943

1. The operation on 25 April 1943, was terminated at 2200 hours. 2. General effects of the execution of this operation.

The Poles resident in Warsaw are much impressed by the toughness of our operation in the former Ghetto. As can be seen from the daily reports, the general situation has greatly calmed down since the beginning of that operation within the city area of Warsaw. From this fact one may conclude that the bandits and saboteurs resided in the former Ghetto, and that now all of them have been destroyed.

In this connection the fact may be of some interest, that an illegal ammunition store was seen to explode when we burned down a certain building in the dwelling area on which we were working at the time.

The SS and Police Fuehrer in the District of Warsaw.
Signed: Stroop

Stalin's Great Terror Violated Communist Principles

NIKITA KHRUSHCHEV

Under the rule of dictator Joseph Stalin, tens of millions of people died in prisons and labor camps, victims of systematic murder and torture precipitated by "enemy purging." Stalin's reign of terror lasted beyond the official years of the Great Terror (1936–1938), yet official Communist Party line held Stalin in highest esteem until a speech by Nikita Khrushchev, excerpted here, marked a major shift in ideology.

Nikita Khrushchev, born in Ukraine in 1894, rose to power through the ranks of the Communist Party. He was appointed Ukrainian prime minister, and in 1953 accepted the position of first secretary of the Soviet Communist Party. In March 1953 the death of Stalin opened the door for either continuation or condemnation of Stalin's policies. On February 24, 1956, Khrushchev addressed the Twentieth Communist Party Congress with a speech highly critical of Stalin's criminal behaviors on the grounds that they were treasonous to party ideology. According to Khrushchev, clear violations of doctrine, such as murdering opponents, hatching sham trials, and rewriting history blatantly violate Communist law. In his argument he illustrates ideological differences between revered leader V.I. Lenin and Stalin to assert that Stalin's use of mass terror was unjustified. Khrushchev, Soviet premier from 1958 to 1964, died in 1971.

Nikita Khrushchev, speech before the Twentieth Congress of the Communist Party of Soviet Russia, February 24 and 25, 1956.

It was precisely during [the years between 1935 and 1938] that the practice of mass repression through the government apparatus was born, first against the enemies of Leninism—Trotskyites,[1] Zinovievites,[2] Bukharinites,[3] long since politically defeated by the Party, and subsequently also against many honest Communists, against those Party cadres who had borne the heavy load of the Civil War[4] and the first and most difficult years of industrialization and collectivization, who actively fought against the Trotskyites and the rightists for the Leninist Party line.

Stalin originated the concept "enemy of the people." This term automatically rendered it unnecessary that the ideological errors of a man or men engaged in a controversy be proven; this term made possible the usage of the most cruel repression, violating all norms of revolutionary legality, against anyone who in any way disagreed with Stalin, against those who were only suspected of hostile intent, against those who had bad reputations. This concept, "enemy of the people," actually eliminated the possibility of any kind of ideological fight or the making of one's views known on this or that issue, even those of a practical character. In the main, and in actuality, the only proof of guilt used, against all norms of current legal science, was the "confession" of the accused himself; and, as subsequent probing proved, "confessions" were acquired through physical pressures against the accused.

Violations of Communist Law

This led to glaring violations of revolutionary legality, and to the fact that many entirely innocent persons, who in the past had defended the Party line, became victims.

We must assert that in regard to those persons who in

1. followers of the form of communism advocated by Leon Trotsky 2. followers of the form of communism advocated by Grigory Zinoviev 3. followers of the form of communism advocated by Nikolai Bukharin 4. After a coup d'etat in October 1917, political divisions in Russia led to Civil War between the Reds (supporters of the new government) and the Whites (those who opposed it).

their time had opposed the Party line, there were often no sufficient serious reasons for their physical annihilation. The formula "enemy of the people" was specifically introduced for the purpose of physically annihilating such individuals.

Differences Between Lenin and Stalin

It is a fact that many persons, who were later annihilated as enemies of the Party and people, had worked with Lenin during his life. Some of these persons had made errors during Lenin's life, but, despite this, Lenin benefited by their work, he corrected them and he did everything possible to retain them in the ranks of the Party; he induced them to follow him. . . .

An entirely different relationship with people characterized Stalin. Lenin's traits—patient work with people; stubborn and painstaking education of them; the ability to induce people to follow him without using compulsion, but rather through the ideological influence on them of the whole collective—were entirely foreign to Stalin. He (Stalin) discarded the Leninist method of convincing and educating; he abandoned the method of ideological struggle for that of administrative violence, mass repressions, and terror. He acted on an increasingly larger scale and more stubbornly through punitive organs, at the same time often violating all existing norms of morality and of Soviet laws.

Arbitrary behavior by one person encouraged and permitted arbitrariness in others. Mass arrests and deportations of many thousands of people; execution without trial and without normal investigation created conditions of insecurity, fear and even desperation.

This, of course, did not contribute toward unity of the Party ranks and of all strata of working people, but on the contrary brought about annihilation and the expulsion from the Party of workers who were loyal but inconvenient to Stalin.

Our Party fought for the implementation of Lenin's plans for the construction of Socialism. This was an ideological fight. Had Leninist principles been observed during the course of this fight, had the Party's devotion to principles been skillfully combined with a keen and solicitous concern for people, had they not been repelled and wasted but rather drawn to our side—we certainly would not have had such a brutal violation of revolutionary legality and many thousands of people would not have fallen victim of the method of terror. Extraordinary methods would then have been resorted to only against those people who had in fact committed criminal acts against the Soviet system. . . .

Lenin used severe methods only in the most necessary cases, when the exploiting classes were still in existence and were vigorously opposing the revolution, when the struggle for survival was decidedly assuming the sharpest forms, even including a civil war.

Stalin, on the other hand, used extreme methods and mass repressions at a time when the revolution was already victorious, when the Soviet state was strengthened, when the exploiting classes were already liquidated and Socialist relations were rooted solidly in all phases of national economy, when our Party was politically consolidated and had strengthened itself both numerically and ideologically. It is clear that here Stalin showed in a whole series of cases his intolerance, his brutality and his abuse of power. Instead of proving his political correctness and mobilizing the masses, he often chose the path of repression and physical annihilation, not only against actual enemies, but also against individuals who had not committed any crimes against the Party and the Soviet government. . . .

Treason Against the Communist Party

Were our Party's holy Leninist principles observed after the death of Vladimir Ilyich? . . .

In practice Stalin ignored the norms of Party life and trampled on the Leninist principle of collective Party leadership. . . .

On the evening of 1 December 1934 on Stalin's initiative

(without the approval of the Political Bureau—which was passed two days later, casually) the secretary of the Presidium of the Central Executive Committee, Yenukidze, signed the following directive.

"I. Investigative agencies are directed to speed up the cases of those accused of the preparation or execution of acts of terror.

"II. Judicial organs are directed not to hold up the execution of death sentences pertaining to crimes of this category in order to consider the possibility of pardon, because the Presidium of the Central Executive Committee USSR does not consider as possible the receiving of petitions of this sort.

"III. The organs of the Commissariat of Internal Affairs are directed to execute the death sentences against criminals of the above-mentioned category immediately after the passage of sentences."

This directive became the basis for mass acts of abuse against Socialist legality. During many of the fabricated court cases the accused were charged with "the preparation" of terroristic acts; this deprived them of any possibility that their cases might be re-examined, even when they stated before the court that their "confessions" were secured by force, and when, in a convincing manner, they disproved the accusations against them. . . .

Stalin's Use of Mass Terror Is Unjustified

Stalin's report at the February–March Central Committee Plenum in 1937, "Deficiencies of Party work and methods for the liquidation of the Trotskyites and of other two-facers," contained an attempt at theoretical justification of the mass terror policy under the pretext that as we march forward toward Socialism class war must allegedly sharpen. Stalin asserted that both history and Lenin taught him this.

Actually Lenin taught that the application of revolutionary violence is necessitated by the resistance of the exploiting classes, and this referred to the era when the exploiting classes existed and were powerful. As soon as the nation's political situation had improved, when in January 1920 the Red Army took Rostov and thus won a most important victory over Denikin,[5] Lenin instructed Dzherzhinsky[6] to stop mass terror and to abolish the death penalty. Lenin justified this important political move of the Soviet State in the following manner in his report at the session of the All-Union Central Executive Committee on 2 February 1920:

"We were forced to use terror because of the terror practiced by the Entente,[7] when strong world powers threw their hordes against us, not avoiding any type of conduct. We would not have lasted two days had we not answered these attempts of officers and White Guardists[8] in a merciless fashion; this meant the use of terror, but this was forced upon us by the terrorist methods of the Entente.

"But as soon as we attained a decisive victory, even before the end of the war, immediately after taking Rostov, we gave up the use of the death penalty and thus proved that we intend to execute our own program in the manner that we promised. We say that the application of violence flows out of the decision to smother the exploiters, the big landowners and the capitalists; as soon as this was accomplished we gave up the use of all extraordinary methods. We have proved this in practice."

5. Anton I. Denikin, tsarist counterrevolutionary in the Civil War   6. Felix Dzherzhinsky, head of secret police   7. collective military action   8. military opponents of Lenin's communism

CHAPTER 3

Terror in the Name of National Liberation

Terror in Opposition to Colonial Rule

ALGERIAN NATIONAL LIBERATION FRONT

The Algerian National Liberation Front (FLN) is an Algerian Socialist political party with terrorist roots that formed in opposition to French colonial rule. Algerian independence was achieved only after eight bloody years (1954–1962) of guerrilla war and terrorism by both the FLN and the French army. The FLN effectively organized insurgents through labor unions and student organizations while it battled rival rebel groups in bloody "café wars" over who would control Algeria's future after the revolution. In August 1955 the FLN killed 123 civilians (including children and the elderly) in a dramatic escalation of violence near Philippeville. Ambushes, night raids, and kidnappings were common tactics of the FLN, as well as torture and murder of captured French forces. Support for pro-independence fighters and the FLN evolved into a sophisticated army of nearly forty thousand troops. In this 1954 proclamation the FLN states its goals for the future of Algeria. It calls for "struggle by every means" to achieve independence.

PROCLAMATION OF THE ALGERIAN NATIONAL LIBERATION FRONT, (FLN) NOVEMBER 1 1954

To the Algerian People! To the militants of the National Cause! After decades of struggle, the National Movement has reached its final phase of fulfilment. At home, the people are united behind the watchwords of independence

---

Algerian National Liberation Front, "Proclamation of the Algerian National Liberation Front," November 1, 1954.

and action. Abroad, the atmosphere is favourable, especially with the diplomatic support of our Arab and Moslem brothers. Our National Movement, prostrated by years of immobility and routine, badly directed was disintegrating little by little. Faced with this situation, a youthful group, gathering about it the majority of wholesome and resolute elements, judged that the moment had come to take the National Movement out of the impasse into which it had been forced by the conflicts of persons and of influence and to launch it into the true revolutionary struggle at the side of the Moroccan and Tunisian brothers. We are independent of the two factions that are vying for power. Our movement gives to compatriots of every social position, to all the purely Algerian parties and movements, the possibility of joining in the liberation struggle.

GOAL: National independence through 1) the restoration of the Algerian state, sovereign, democratic, and social, within the framework of the principles of Islam; 2) the preservation of fundamental freedoms, without distinction of race or religion.

INTERNAL Objectives: Political house-cleaning through the destruction of the last vestiges of corruption and reformism.

EXTERNAL Objectives: 1) The internationalization of the Algerian problem; 2) The pursuit of North African unity in its national Arabo-Islamic context; 3) The assertion, through United Nations channels, of our active sympathy toward all nations that may support our liberating action.

MEANS OF STRUGGLE: Struggle by every means until our goal is attained. Exertion at home and abroad through political and direct action, with a view to making the Algerian problem a reality for the entire world. The struggle will be long, but the outcome is certain. To limit the bloodshed, we propose an honourable platform for discussion with the French authorities: 1) The opening of negotiations with the authorized spokesmen the Algerian people, on the basis of a recognition of Algerian sovereignty, one and indivisible. 2) The inception of an atmosphere of confidence brought about freeing all those who are detained, by annulling all measures exception, and by ending all legal action against the combatant forces. 3) The recognition of Algerian nationhood by an official declaration abrogating all edicts, decrees, and laws by virtue of which Algeria was "French soil."

In return for which: 1) French cultural and economic interests will be respected, as well as persons and families. 2) All French citizens desiring to remain in Algeria will be allowed to opt for their original nationality, in which case they will be considered as foreigners, or for Algerian nationality, in which case they will be considered as Algerians, equal both as to rights and as to duties. 3) The ties between France and Algeria will be the object of agreement between the two Powers on the basis of equality and mutual respect. Algerians: The F.L.N. is your front; its victory is your victory. For our part, strong in your support, we shall give the best of ourselves to the Fatherland.

Terrorism in the Struggle for Israel

MENACHEM BEGIN

At the end of World War I the League of Nations gave control of Eretz Israel (the territory of modern-day Israel) to the United Kingdom in what is known as the British mandate of Palestine. Controversial British policies on key issues such as immigration and land ownership fueled violence between Jews and Arabs and triggered the formation of anti-British militias such as the Jewish terrorist group Irgun Zva'i Le'umi (Irgun).

Menachem Begin, a former member of Irgun, was born in Poland in 1913, and by the age of twenty-four he had successfully organized protests of British policy in Palestine. He and other activists entered Palestine as illegal immigrants to work as operatives, and in 1943 Begin rose to the head of the Irgun organization. In this chapter from his 1951 book The Revolt, *Begin describes working with operatives named Sneh, Galili, and Giddy as they execute the 1946 terrorist bombing of the King David Hotel, which was a British military headquarters. Although they were warned of the impending attack, the British failed to evacuate the hotel, and ninety-one people were killed. Forty-five more were injured. Begin considers the deaths of innocent civilians a tragedy and concludes that victory has been marred by the loss of innocents. Begin was prime minister of Israel from 1977 to 1983. He died in 1992.*

During World War II the southern wing of the King David Hotel in Jerusalem was taken over to house the central institutions of the British regime: Military G.H.Q., and the Secretariat, the civil Government. As the revolt against British rule intensified, the great hotel was developed into a veritable fortress in the heart of the city. In a neighbouring building, the British Military Police and the famous Special Investigation Bureau established their headquarters. In the open space between the two buildings a strong military unit was encamped. Machine-gun nests were constructed at a number of points. Soldiers, police and detectives maintained a close and constant watch on the building which housed the supreme British rulers in Eretz Israel. . . .

The host of watching eyes surrounding the King David Hotel saw nothing of our reconnaissance—the messengers of the underground remained unseen, but saw what they had to see, and found out what they sought. The plan for an attack on the King David Hotel began to take shape.

Rules for the Attack

In the Spring of 1946 we submitted our plan for the first time to the Command of the Resistance Movement. I informed Sneh and Galili that we would undertake to penetrate the Government wing of the King David Hotel and to carry out an extensive sabotage operation. Without going into details, I emphasized that the employment of explosives would be distinguished by a new device, invented by Giddy. On the one hand our "mines" could not be moved or dismantled as they would blow up on contact. On the other hand we would be able to fix the moment for the explosion of these "mines" by a time mechanism, half-an-hour or even an hour after their introduction into the building. This would allow for evacuation by hotel guests, workers and officials. The rules we had laid down for ourselves made the evacuation of the hotel essential. There were many civilians in the hotel whom we wanted, at all costs, to avoid injuring. We were anxious to ensure that they should leave the danger zone in plenty of time for their safety.

The Haganah Command [underground military body of Jews in Eretz Israel] did not at once approve our plan. They regarded an attack on the headquarters of British rule as too ambitious. They were not against it in principle. They argued that the time had not yet come for such an attack, which was likely to inflame the British excessively. We thought otherwise, but were bound by our agreement and had to bow to their decision. But we did not give up our plan. In our personal talks with the Haganah chiefs . . . we put forward the plan anew. Our code name for the great King David Hotel was at first "Malonchik" ("little hotel"). Later, to improve the camouflage we all called it "Chick.". . . .

Doctrinaire reasoning ("the scope of the reprisal is equal to the magnitude of the attack") [by the Haganah] led to the approval of our plan to attack the King David Hotel. On the 29th of June 1946 the British occupied the Offices of the Jewish Agency. The Jewish Agency was regarded as "Jewish headquarters." So, according to the doctrinaire argument we must repay them in kind and attack *their* headquarters, in the King David Hotel.

Further Impetus for the Attack

The second reason was a more serious one. The Haganah, which had become accustomed to its convenient "semilegal" status in the eyes of the British authorities, had never taken efficient steps to observe the rules of caution. The Jewish Agency leaders apparently put their trust in their imagined "international status" which they fondly believed gave them immunity from police action. Consequently there were many secret documents in the Jewish Agency building which a wisely run organisation in such circumstances would never have allowed to be there. The booty which the British forces carried away as a result of their searches in the Jewish Agency building was considerable. The irresponsibility that prevailed in the Jewish Agency reached such a pitch that, as Galili told me, the

British were able to take out of a typewriter part of the verbatim report of Mr. [Moishe] Shertok's [first foreign minister of Israel] speech at the Zionist General Council. Mr. Shertok had praised the blowing-up of the bridges, and explained the great political significance of the operation.

The report of Shertok's speech, which corroborated Jewish Agency responsibility for the Haganah's sabotage operations, gave the lie to the emphatic disclaimers Mr. [David] Ben Gurion [prime minister of Israel 1948–1953, 1955–1963] had made before the Anglo-American Commission only a few months previously. It was not the only document of this kind which the British carried away to the King David Hotel.

Anxiety for the destruction of these documents was plainly indicated at the meeting between Yitshak Sadeh, the Operations officer of the Haganah, and our Giddy. Yitshak Sadeh asked Giddy how much time he was allowing between the introduction of the explosives into the building and the explosion. Giddy suggested forty-five minutes. Sadeh thought this was "too long, as the British might then manage not only to evacuate their people *but to get the documents out as well.*" He consequently proposed that we allow only fifteen minutes for the evacuation of the hotel. Giddy reassured him. Despite his youth Giddy had had far more practical experience in this kind of fighting than had the Haganah Operations officer. He replied that experience had taught him that when the authorities received warning that one of their offices was about to be blown up, they left the building at high speed, and did not waste time on documents. Giddy felt that fifteen minutes might not give a safe margin for evacuating the building. Finally, agreement was reached by a compromise: half-an-hour. . . .

An "Unprecedented" Attack in Scope

We were well aware that this was the largest of our operations to date and that it might turn out to be unique in the history of partisan wars of liberation. It is no simple matter to penetrate the very heart of the military government, to deliver a blow within the fortified headquarters of a heavily armed regime. I doubt if this operation had any precedent in history.

We dared not fail. After the 29th of June [attack on the Jewish Agency], large sections of the people had been thrown into confusion. . . . Defeatism raised its deathly head. People began to question our ability to fight the British regime. Many expressed their despair as to the outcome of any "struggle": "Who are we, what is our strength, that we should be able to stand up to the British Army?" These questions were pregnant with danger. They reflected the defeatism that is fatal to every war of liberation. We realised that Jewish self-confidence could be restored only by a successful counter-attack. . . .

Giddy's tremendous inventive and creative powers were called upon to the full. Innocent milk-cans became the bearers of high explosives. Their action was doubly assured. One mechanism determined the time of explosion—half-an-hour after the cans were left in position; the other secured the cans against any attempt at removal or dismantling.

A prime consideration was the timing of the attack. Two proposals were made: one for eleven A.M., the other for between four and five o'clock in the afternoon. Both plans were based on the same reasoning. The milk-cans could be brought into the Government wing of the building only by way of the "Regence Café" situated in the basement of the wing occupied by Barker[1] and Shaw.[2] In these morning and afternoon hours the Café was usually empty. At lunch-time it was filled with customers, among them civilian men and women as well as Army officers. It was essential that the attack be delivered at an hour when there were no customers in the Café.

---

1. General Sir Evelyn Barker, British army commander in Palestine   2. Sir John Shaw, chief secretary for the government of Palestine

Of the proposed hours, which both met this condition, we chose the earlier—11 A.M. . . .

Next we considered how to give the warnings so as to eliminate casualties. First, to keep passers-by away from the building, we decided to let off a small cracker-bomb, noisy but harmless. Then we chose three offices to receive a telephoned warning, which would be given as soon as our men had got away from the basement of the hotel. These three were: the King David Hotel management; the *Palestine Post*, and the French Consulate-General which is close to the Hotel. Finally, warning placards would be placed next to the milk-cans: "Mines. Do not Touch"—in case British experts should attempt to dismantle the explosives after our telephoned warning had been sent out. . . .

Because of last-minute consultations, the time of attack was delayed by one hour and began at twelve o'clock instead of eleven.

The Execution of "Operation Chick"

The Assault Unit, under the command of the Jerusalem Gideon (dressed in the flowing robes of a hotel worker), executed the attack with great bravery and carried out their orders with absolute punctiliousness. They brought the milk-cans as far as the approach to the hotel. They then divided into two groups, one for the "break-through" and the other to "cover" the first. The first group took the milk-cans into the basement by way of the Regence Café. They overwhelmed the café employees and locked them in a side-room. These fifteen Arabs presented no surprise to our men: the peaceful subjection of the cooks and waiters—the only persons in the café at the time—was part of the plan. But our men were surprised by the sudden appearance of two British soldiers who, their suspicions being aroused, drew their revolvers. A clash was unavoidable. Both sides suffered casualties. Meanwhile the covering group outside had clashed with the British military patrols. In view of the nature of the operation our men had no machine-guns and had to fight with sten-guns and revolvers. However, the break-through party reached its objective. The commander of the operation himself set the time mechanism at thirty minutes and put up the warning placards. The Arab workers were then freed and ordered to run for their lives. They did not hesitate. The last man out was Gideon, who shouted "Get away, the hotel is about to blow up." At the moment the warning cracker-bomb was exploded outside the hotel and under cover of its smoke our men withdrew. The noise caused by the bomb and the unexpected shooting drove away all passers-by in the streets.

At ten minutes past twelve, Gideon reached the spot at which our "telephonist" was waiting. She immediately telephoned the King David Hotel and warned them that explosives had been placed under the hotel and would go off within a short time. "Evacuate the whole building!"—she cried to the hotel telephone-operator. She then telephoned the office of the *Palestine Post* and announced—as was later testified by the *Palestine Post* telephonist—that "bombs have been placed in the King David Hotel and the people there have been told to evacuate the building." The third and final warning was given to the French Consulate, accompanied by advice to open the Consulate windows so as to prevent the effects of blast. The Consulate officials subsequently confirmed the receipt of the warning. They opened their windows wide, and the French Consulate building suffered no damage.

It was now twelve-fifteen. Gideon was counting the minutes. So far, everything had gone according to plan, except for the casualties we had suffered in the unexpected clash. The milk-cans were lodged in the basement under the Government wing of the hotel. All warnings had been delivered and received. The British had no doubt begun the evacuation and, if things had gone as before in similar circumstances, would very soon complete it. Only one question bothered him: would the explosives go off? Might not some error have been made in the mechanism? Would the building really go up? Would the documents be destroyed?

Each minute seemed like a day. Twelve-thirty-one, thirty-two. Zero hour drew near. Gideon grew restless. The half-hour was almost up. Twelve-thirty-seven. . . . Suddenly, the whole town seemed to shudder. There had been no mistake. The force of the explosion was greater than had been expected. Yitshak Sadeh, of the Haganah, had doubted whether it would reach the third or even the second floor. Giddy had claimed that, though only about 500 lbs. of explosives—a compound of T.N.T. and gelignite—had been put into the milk-cans, the confined space of the basement would heighten the force of the escaping gases, and the explosion would reach the roof. The milk-cans "reached" the whole height of the building, from basement to roof, six storeys of stone, concrete and steel. As the B.B.C. put it— the entire wing of a huge building was cut off as with a knife.

But while our Assault Unit in the lion's den had done everything possible to ensure the timely evacuation of the hotel, others had taken a different line. For some reason the hotel was not evacuated even though from the moment when the warnings had been received there was plenty of time for every living soul to saunter out. Instead, the toll of lives was terrible. More than two hundred people were killed or injured. Among the victims were high British officers. We particularly mourned the alien civilians whom we had had no wish to hurt, and the fifteen Jewish civilians, among them good friends, who had so tragically fallen. Our satisfaction at the success of the great operation was bitterly marred. Again we went through days of pain and nights of sorrow for the blood that need not have been shed.

Palestinian Revolutionaries Are Freedom Fighters, Not Terrorists

YASIR ARAFAT

In the aftermath of World War I the British mandate of Palestine physically dispossessed property-owning Palestinians, facilitated an influx of Jewish immigration, and infuriated Arabs. The dispute over Palestinian-Israeli borders and property rights continues to this day in an ongoing cycle of violence in the Middle East.

Yasir Arafat became leader of the Palestine Liberation Organization (PLO), a group that was originally dedicated to the forceful dissolution of Israel, in 1968. The PLO was responsible for many terrorist attacks. On November 13, 1974, Arafat answered an invitation to speak before the United Nations General Assembly. Addressing the role of his organization in the violence between Jews and Arabs, he contends that the PLO has been unfairly labeled a terrorist group. He insists that the Palestinian people have been robbed of their homeland and are justified in their quest to reclaim it. By framing this issue as a moral quest for freedom, he rejects for himself and his supporters the label of terrorist. In his closing statements Arafat warns that his supporters will resort to violence if Palestinian occupation continues. His address emboldened Palestinians in Israel, and as a result, several mili-

Yasir Arafat, address before the UN General Assembly, November 13, 1974.

tant groups launched attacks against Israeli troops.

*Arafat remains chairman of the PLO. Although his organi-
zation disavows the use of violence, its critics claim that it
tacitly endorses, and thereby encourages, terrorism against
Israel.*

This is a very important occasion. The question of Palestine is being reexamined by the United Nations, and we
consider that step to be a victory for the world organization as much as a victory for the cause of our people. It indicates anew that the United Nations of today is not the
United Nations of the past, just as today's world is not yesterday's world. Today's United Nations represents 138 nations, a number that more clearly reflects the will of the international community. Thus today's United Nations is
more nearly capable of implementing the principles em-
bodied in its Charter and in the Universal Declaration of
Human Rights, as well as being more truly empowered to
support causes of peace and justice. . . .

The roots of the Palestinian question reach back into the
closing years of the 19th century, in other words, to that
period which we call the era of colonialism and settlement
as we know it today. This is precisely the period during
which Zionism as a scheme was born. Its aim was the conquest of Palestine by European immigrants, just as settlers
colonized, and indeed raided, most of Africa. This is the period during which, pouring forth out of the west, colonialism spread into the furthest reaches of Africa, Asia, and
Latin America, building colonies, everywhere cruelly exploiting, oppressing, plundering the peoples of those three
continents. . . .

Palestine Is Our Homeland

As a result of the collusion between the mandatory Power
[Great Britain] and the Zionist movement and with the support of some countries, this General Assembly early in its

history approved a recommendation to partition our Palestinian homeland. This took place in an atmosphere poisoned with questionable actions and strong pressure. The General Assembly partitioned what it had no right to divide—an indivisible homeland. When we rejected that decision, our position corresponded to that of the natural mother who refused to permit King Solomon to cut her son in two when the unnatural mother claimed the child for herself and agreed to his dismemberment. Furthermore, even though the partition resolution granted the colonialist settlers 54 percent of the land of Palestine, their dissatisfaction with the decision prompted them to wage a war of terror against the civilian Arab population. They occupied 81 per cent of the total area of Palestine, uprooting a million Arabs. Thus they occupied 524 Arab towns and villages, of which they destroyed 385, completely obliterating them in the process. Having done so, they built their own settlements and colonies on the ruins of our farms and our groves. The roots of the Palestine question lie here. Its causes do not stem from any conflict between two religions or two nationalisms. Neither is it a border conflict between neighboring states. It is the cause of people deprived of its homeland, dispersed and uprooted, and living mostly in exile and in refugee camps. . . .

It pains our people greatly to witness the propagation of the myth that its homeland was a desert until it was made to bloom by the toil of foreign settlers, that it was a land without a people, and that the colonialist entity caused no harm to any human being. No: such lies must be exposed from this rostrum, for the world must know that Palestine was the cradle of the most ancient cultures and civilizations. Its Arab people were engaged in farming and building, spreading culture throughout the land for thousands of years, setting an example in the practice of freedom of worship, acting as faithful guardians of the holy places of all religions. . . .

If the immigration of Jews to Palestine had had as its objective the goal of enabling them to live side by side with us, enjoying the same rights and assuming the same duties, we would have opened our doors to them, as far as our homeland's capacity for absorption permitted. Such was the case with the thousands of Armenians and Circassians who still live among us in equality as brethren and citizens. But that the goal of this immigration should be to usurp our homeland, disperse our people, and turn us into second-class citizens—this is what no one can conceivably demand that we acquiesce in or submit to. Therefore, since its inception, our revolution has not been motivated by racial or religious factors. Its target has never been the Jew, as a person, but racist Zionism and undisguised aggression. In this sense, ours is also a revolution for the Jew, as a human being, as well. We are struggling so that Jews, Christians, and Muslims may live in equality, enjoying the same rights and assuming the same duties, free from racial or religious discrimination. . . .

Those who call us terrorists wish to prevent world public opinion from discovering the truth about us and from seeing the justice on our faces. They seek to hide the terrorism and tyranny of their acts, and our own posture of self defense.

The difference between the revolutionary and the terrorist lies in the reason for which each fights. For whoever stands by a just cause and fights for the freedom and liberation of his land from the invaders, the settlers, and the colonialists cannot possibly be called terrorist, otherwise the American people in their struggle for liberation from the British colonialists would have been terrorists, the European resistance against the Nazis would be terrorism, the struggle of the Asian, African, and Latin American peoples would also be terrorism, and many of you who are in this Assembly hall were considered terrorists. This is actually a just and proper struggle consecrated by the United Nations Charter and by the Universal Declaration of Human Rights. As to those who fight against the just causes, those who wage war to occupy, colonize, and oppress other people, those are the terrorists. Those are the people whose actions should be condemned, who should be called war criminals: for the justice of the cause determines the right to struggle.

Zionist terrorism which was waged against the Palestinian people to evict it from its country and usurp its land is registered in our official documents. Thousands of our people were assassinated in their villages and towns, tens of thousands of others were forced at gunpoint to leave their homes and the lands of their fathers. Time and time again our children, women, and aged were evicted and had to wander in the deserts and climb mountains without any food or water. No one who in 1948 witnessed the catastrophe that befell the inhabitants of hundreds of villages and towns—in Jerusalem, Jaffa, Lydda, Ramle, and Galilee—no one who has been a witness to that catastrophe will ever forget the experience, even though the mass blackout has succeeded in hiding these horrors as it has hidden the traces of 385 Palestinian villages and towns destroyed at the time and erased from the map. The destruction of 19,000 houses during the past seven years, which is equivalent to the complete destruction of 200 more Palestinian villages, and the great number of maimed as a result of the treatment they were subjected to in Israeli prisons, cannot be hidden by any blackout. . . .

Need one remind this Assembly of the numerous resolutions adopted by it condemning Israeli aggressions committed against Arab countries, Israeli violations of human rights, and the articles of the Geneva Conventions, as well as the resolutions pertaining to the annexation of the city of Jerusalem and its restoration to its former status?

The only description for these acts is that they are acts of barbarism and terrorism. And yet, the Zionist racists and colonialists have the temerity to describe the just struggle of our people as terror. Could there be a more flagrant distortion of truth than this? . . .

A Freedom Fighter

I am a rebel and freedom is my cause. I know well that many of you present here today once stood in exactly the same resistance position as I now occupy and from which I must fight. You once had to convert dreams into reality by your struggle. Therefore you must now share my dream. . . .

In my formal capacity as Chairman of the Palestine Liberation Organization and leader of the Palestinian revolution I appeal to you to accompany our people in its struggle to attain its right to self-determination. This right is consecrated in the United Nations Charter and has been repeatedly confirmed in resolutions adopted by this august body since the drafting of the Charter. I appeal to you, further, to aid our people's return to its homeland from an involuntary exile imposed upon it by force of arms, by tyranny, by oppression, so that we may regain our property, our land, and thereafter live in our national homeland, free and sovereign, enjoying all the privileges of nationhood. Only then can we pour all our resources into the mainstream of human civilization. Only then can Palestinian creativity be concentrated on the service of humanity. Only then will our Jerusalem resume its historic role as a peaceful shrine for all religions.

I appeal to you to enable our people to establish national independent sovereignty over its own land.

Today I have come bearing an olive branch and a freedom fighter's gun. Do not let the olive branch fall from my hand. I repeat: Do not let the olive branch fall from my hand.

Taking Up Arms for Irish Independence

LAWRENCE MCKEOWN

The Irish Republican Army (IRA) is an organization devoted to the creation of a unified Ireland free of British rule. The IRA has gone through many incarnations in its history, and splinter groups such as the Provisional IRA have formed in the years since its inception. In 1949 the southern (mainly Catholic) part of Ireland achieved independence, yet Northern Ireland (mainly Protestant) remained a British province. Tensions between Catholics and Protestants in Northern Ireland escalated after Bloody Sunday, January 30, 1972, when British soldiers gunned down thirteen Catholic marchers. Throughout its history, the IRA has, at various times and to various degrees, used terrorism—including bombings and kidnapping—to pursue its goal of independence. Lawrence McKeown is a former IRA member who participated in bombings and hunger strike. In the following excerpt from a 1997 interview, he explains that the terrors he perpetrated, as well as his arrest and imprisonment, were all worthwhile experiences.

I lived out in the country outside Randalstown so it was fairly quiet. I would have had an upbringing that was in a neighbourhood that was mixed. There was absolutely no sectarian element at that stage. Randalstown was seen as predominantly Protestant yet Catholics owned 50 per cent of premises.

I think it was after the formation of the UDR [Ulster Defence Regiment of the British Army]. A number of ones we drank with were suddenly in the UDR, and coming home at night, getting stopped by them, and then the ridiculous thing of them asking you your name, which, one night, when it first happened, turned into a laugh from ourselves in the car. But we seen fairly quickly that the ones who were asking it weren't seeing it as a laugh. I felt physically afraid of some areas or if you were stopped at night by the UDR you were very much conscious that this was like a Protestant Loyalist force. You had things like UDA [the British loyalist Ulster Defence Association] in Randalstown and they became much more physical, so you would have felt under threat.

Patterns would have changed. We stopped drinking in Randalstown. You would have changed your route coming back from different places. You became very much aware what were safe areas.

Joining the IRA

I had thought about it. I was singing these [Republican] songs and talking and discussing what was going on about our defence and at the same time not playing any active part. So, I came to the decision to join the IRA, but it was a long thought out one and the process of getting into it was also a long one.

It was about a couple of months later that someone approached me one night. They had created a situation where I was with them and they said they had heard I was interested in joining the IRA and that the IRA at that time was interested in forming a unit in the area I lived in. I said I definitely was, and that took a procedure which took probably seven to eight months, to the point where I was getting exasperated, thinking that somebody had forgotten about me, that I wasn't moving ahead.

But then I was taken in and asked again by others in a more formal situation had I thought it out and was I aware of the consequences and to rethink my position, the fears of imprisonment, or being shot or killed or whatever. I said that I had thought of a lot of those issues that they had raised, that I didn't think I was going to change my mind. So, they said to give it some more thought but I didn't change my mind. Shortly after that I ended up in the IRA.

IRA Operations

Whenever I became active in the IRA the operations carried out were always kept outside of the area so it wasn't too difficult to get out of the house to do things. I was seventeen at the time. After one operation where a car had to be hijacked, I had to then drive it to go down the road to pick up a bomb and bring it back up again. So, to go down the road I had to take the mask off and I didn't know at the time that the car had been seen getting hijacked. So, there was this crowd of people seen me and one of them knew me from school.

When the bomb went off in Randalstown my name started to be mentioned in a bar, so there was a lot of discussion about what we should do. I went home and my parents were out. I didn't know where they were—they were actually in a neighbour's house—but I saw another neighbour and I called her aside and said that I had to leave, that I was involved in that last bomb explosion in Randalstown and apparently I had been spotted and my name was out. I suppose it was a bit of a rush once the decision was taken. We were more aware of getting out immediately. So, I left and stayed round Toomebridge that night and next day was moved over the border into Monaghan.

It often seems very scary, but bombs, until they're primed, you can practically do anything with them so it's not as if you're sort of sitting waiting for something constantly to go off. Right enough, in those days the timing mechanisms were much more crude therefore liable to accidentally being put off. But if you were anyway careful at all you could totally reduce that. I suppose there's more of an acceleration, there's adrenaline once you're doing anything. I think anybody, should they be British soldiers or whatever else, once the operation is happening you're powered on by something that doesn't normally sort of propel you.

Life on the Run

In 1973 or 1974, it would have been a fairly loose chain of command that I would have been coming into contact with. I mean, you certainly had your immediate superiors. There would have been infrequent meetings with them and the meetings would have been fairly informal. People got to know one another and each one had a role to do but there was a fair degree of independence.

Shortly after that I contacted my family and met with my mother and sister down in Monaghan, which was strained. I suppose she was concerned how I was and what was happening. The whole relationship I had with her afterward— she never really condemned me for what I was doing. I think my father would have been more disappointed. I had met him briefly, we only spent a couple of weeks together, but it was a fairly strained. I know he didn't agree with my politics or what I had done.

You ended up you had no money, you were staying in people's houses who were actually just keeping you. You were unsettled being there, you preferred to be in the North. Any romantic notions about being on the run very quickly disappeared. The contact with the unit stopped as soon as I left but it didn't stop with the IRA because they always had a structure in Monaghan and a structure which was tied in with people who were on the run, that was maintained.

I argued for an attack upon, well it could have been the British Army, RUC [Royal Ulster Constabulary police force], UDR or whatever. It would be like a military patrol and it ended up I was on it myself. It was a July night it happened on, finally.

The attack was on an RUC Land Rover—one policeman

was injured very slightly. But it was fairly close to even my own home. And then I was out of the house after that. Anyway, one night I ended up coming back to the house, it was on a Sunday night and the next morning it was raided. I was arrested and taken to Castlereagh, interrogated and charged with attempted murder and causing explosions previously. . . .

The court lasted two days, it was just dragging out all this. Somebody in the army tactical had to say, 'Yes, this explosion actually happened.' It was that sort of evidence rather than eyewitnesses. So, it lasted one full day and the next morning and then I was sentenced that morning before dinner-time for five counts of life. I got four hundred years. I was just relieved it was over.

You knew you were going to be sentenced, you knew you were going to be in the protest [hunger strike] and you actually wanted to be down and be on it. . . .

Hunger Strikes

I never wanted to leave the protest, simply because it was right I should be there. There had always been talk about a hunger strike, simply because within Republican history, in prison hunger strike had always been the ultimate. The decision had always been to try and exhaust every other means first. At one time in 1980 it was thought we were going to get our own clothes, which really would have ended the protest because that was the major thing. The uniform was the badge of criminalisation. It was felt that most of that had been exhausted, in terms of outside protesting and media coverage, so it was then decided that there would be a hunger strike. People were asked to put forward their names but there was seven people selected for it. . . .

I put my name forward. I was young, I wasn't married and I didn't have children. I believed that it was right, that everything else had been exhausted. A lot of people can't understand the hunger strikes without realising the years that went before it, that you are totally incarcerated in a cell twenty-four hours a day—you are in those conditions and that's the battle on it. I was doing life imprisonment so it was like the future of my life. The first hunger strike had ended after fifty-three days and on the fiftieth day there had been another group of thirty people joined the hunger strike and I was one of them. So, that night there was all the talk about what was going to happen in the morning and all this sort of exhilaration.

First thing in the morning, the doors were opened and some NIO [Northern Ireland Office] official threw in this leaflet. There was a discussion about this document and it had been agreed there was enough in this foggy language that would resolve it and move us out of that situation. But within a couple of days, because there was no movement at all and suspicion set in very quickly. It was apparent that . . . there was [not] going to be any big change. We were sitting exactly as we had been prior to the ending of the hunger strike. We knew something was going badly wrong. I think that was the worst time I ever spent in jail. . . .

The second hunger strike started really slowly. . . .

You drank ten pints of water a day. It was cold water and at that time of the year the heating was off in the Blocks so coldness was the only thing I would have felt. You never really lose the appetite—the food you were getting was terrible, but because you knew you weren't going to eat anything you didn't have that same feeling of hunger. Yes you felt an emptiness in your stomach for the first few days and after that your stomach starts to shrink down. After the fortieth day, the eyes started to get fuzzy, you have double vision, and then you wake up blinking into them. . . .

You start out from the position of . . . you hope it's going to end before you die. You do end up thinking, I could die here—but that changes as time goes on. Because you are so focused on the whole thing, what it's about, the necessity of it. The hunger strike is about the rest of your time in jail, if you are beaten on that, you are going to live your life in jail, broken, and they are going to dominate you.

I thought about dying. It didn't frighten me. Maybe you were very sad at the thought that you were going to die and all you are going to lose. You were allowed one visit a week and then, after a while, arranged special visits. Some of the other hunger strikers had a policy at the start of whenever people became ill, allowing the family in to stay with them. I think two members of the family could be there at any one time but it was only really the last three days. . . .

I can understand the situation my mother was in at that time. The whole pressure was on the families. The pressure had moved from the British Government to the families and the whole thought was that no mother could sit there and possibly watch her son die without intervening. Which is what led to the whole position to end the hunger strike, not because volunteers had stopped; there were still people lining up to join the hunger strike after the ten people had died. But it comes to a point where you say, well, it's not achieving anything.

Inside I think I have experienced a type of life—experienced emotions that are deepest. I see life ever afterwards as being an anticlimax because I feel myself that I have lived it to its full, in the sense of being on the edge of the deepest of emotions that you could experience—which are from very negative ones of anger and rage and hate to ones of exhilaration and love and comradeship. You just wouldn't have that sort of degree of comradeship or friendship to the same extent outside. So, I don't look back on it in a negative sense at all.

If I had to live it all over again I would do exactly the same.

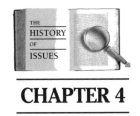

THE
HISTORY
OF
ISSUES

CHAPTER 4

Terrorism and the United States

American Slavery Is a Form of Terrorism

NEW YORK DAILY TIMES

Enslaved peoples in the American South fell victim to many heinous crimes beyond imprisonment and subjugation, with no representation or recourse. Slavery, euphemistically called "The Peculiar Institution" by proponents, amounted to politically sanctioned terrorism. To many abolitionists in the North, the crimes of slavery were political and religious. A reporter from the New York Daily Times *describes the torture and murder of two slaves near a Presbyterian church in eastern Tennessee and concludes that a Christian nation must not tolerate this type of terrorism.*

Eastern Tennessee has had the reputation, for some time past, of being an all but Free-Soil district. Its inhabitants have enjoyed the character of being tolerators rather than admirers of Slavery, of cherishing the good old American doctrine that Slavery is an evil, of which it were well we should rid ourselves at the earliest possible moment, having a due regard to the welfare of the blacks and the serenity of the whites. A recent English traveler, MR. STERLING, speaks of the difference in the feeling on this all important question which he noticed in this region, as compared with others further west. "There was much to please and interest me," he says, "in my progress from East Tennessee to West Virginia; but what pleased and interested me beyond everything else was the positive information I received re-

---

New York Daily Times, "Discouraging to 'Fanatics,'" September 5, 1857.

garding the progress of Abolition sentiments in this region. The truth is, I believe, that Western Virginia, and more or less all the frontier states, have become Abolitionized without knowing it. The spell of Slavery is still so strong in these lands, the old ideas have still so strong a hold on the imagination, if not on the understanding, and the terrorism exercised by the fanatical believers in Slavery is so powerful, that the strength of the heretical element is unknown alike to those who have discarded the old faith, and those who hold by it." MR. OLMSTED, in his preface to MR. GLADSTONE'S "Englishman in Kansas," says of the same district: "There is no part of the South in which the people are more free from the direct action of Slavery on the character, or where they have less to apprehend from rebellion, than Eastern Tennessee."

In spite of this high character, and these favorable antecedents, a thousand of the best citizens of the place, a few years ago, assembled in cold blood and burnt a negro alive at the stake. One of the local papers commenting on the tragedy boasts of the fact,—which in any other civilized community would have been considered an aggravation of the atrocity—that the perpetrators were "cool, calm, and deliberate." The editor of this same journal, "a minister of the Gospel," adds: "We unhesitatingly affirm that the punishment was unequal to the crime. Had we been there, we should have taken a part, and even suggested the pinching of pieces out of him with red-hot pincers, the cutting off of a limb at a time, and then burning them all in a heap." A few days since the place was signalized by another occurrence of a somewhat similar character, and which exemplifies in an equally remarkable manner the nature of the "Christianity" which the inhabitants profess. A certain Col. NETHERLAND, a wealthy member of the Second Presbyterian Church, Rogersville, sold a slave to a trader to be taken down South and separated from his wife and family. The man on hearing of it, very naturally ran away, and succeeded in concealing himself in the woods for a year. He was at last discovered and brought back, and Col. NETHER-LAND, "member of the Second Presbyterian Church," forthwith handed him over to the trader, with a stipulation that he should be "openly and publicly whipped." He was accordingly led past the parsonage, in which Colonel NETHERLAND'S minister resides, to a field hand behind the church in which the same gentleman sits every "Sabbath" at the feet of Him who brought deliverance to the captive and light to the blind. He was there stripped naked, tied on his face to the ground, so that he could move neither hand nor foot, blindfolded, and three hundred and thirty blows were inflicted upon him, the skin breaking at every stroke. This performance took place so very close to the building, that the cries of the tortured victim could be heard in the House of God. They were heard, too, we doubt not, in a holier place than the Rogersville Church.

The Unjustifiability of Torture

In order that nothing should be wanting to make the hideous drama complete, the Colonel handed over an aged negro, one of his own slaves, whom he suspected of having harbored or aided the fugitive, to the same trader, with a request that he would whip him too. The old man was accordingly carried to a neighboring county, and on Sunday morning, he was taken to a hay loft, tied naked on a plank, and then received three hundred blows of the flat of a carpenter's hand saw—Mississippi fashion. Each blow raised blisters, and the next broke them, so that the man's back was flayed.

The Church Session meets, on hearing of this, and sends the Colonel a polite message, at the instigation of the minister, in whom the voice of humanity seems to have still whispered, though in faltering accents, requesting him to come before them, and relieve himself of "unjust censure." He resents this inference as unwarrantable, and finally succeeds in turning the scale in his favor as to drive out the minister, Mr. SAWYER. The congregation sided with the

Colonel, and a writer in a local paper, supposed to be his brother-in-law, defended the whole transaction, remarking, that "if he did whip the negro till he died, he was his money, and there the matter ended."

The best or worst remains to be told. The clergyman, thus expelled for having feebly and faintly performed a duty, which, to him, should have been as sacred as his mother's ashes, and as imperious as if an angel's trumpet had called him to it, in an address published before his departure, prays that God will send them another, and, of course, more pliant pastor, "to build them up a united people"—or, to substitute good Saxon for the jargon of the camp-meeting, to pander to their prejudices, gloss over their sins, and bring on them the curse of the self-deceiver and of the willfully blind. He adds, moreover, that as long as he lives, "as long as he has pen, tongue, or arm, Abolitionism shall find an enemy in him."

We feel thankful that we live in an age in which it is not necessary to argue with the mass of the civilized world upon the justifiability of torture, the expediency of burning alive, or the glories of mob-law. To ask for pity at the bar of Christian public opinion for the sufferings of these two wretched negroes, for indignation on the head of him who caused them, would be as much a work of supererogation as to pray that the tide might ebb and flow, or that the sun might rise on the morrow.

The 1960s Counterculture Gave Rise to Leftist Terrorists

EHUD SPRINZAK

During the 1960s people who were politically, socially, and otherwise critical of mainstream values and thought were considered part of the American counterculture. From this subsection of society emerged a student movement called the New Left that argued for societal awareness of the perils of affluence and capitalism. One of the New Left's most visible organizations was the nonviolent Students for a Democratic Society (SDS). A radicalized splinter faction of the SDS, known as the Weathermen, advocated the violent overthrow of the U.S. government. From 1969 to 1976 the Weathermen waged a terror campaign of riots, violent uprisings, and bombings. Why these political radicals rejected social protest in lieu of bloody ideological terrorism is a question that scholar and terrorism expert Ehud Sprinzak contemplates in the following selection. Sprinzak served as an adviser to Israeli prime minister Yitzak Rabin and authored several works on right-wing Israeli extremism.

On 7 October 1969, a blast destroyed a police monument in Chicago. Two days later, leaflets were circulated in that city by a small radical organization, the Weatherman, announcing four days of "national action" against the war in Vietnam. This action, the citizens of Chicago were told, would include a mass rally, an attack on the Chicago Armed Forces Induction Center by the "Women's Militia," demonstrations at high schools, a "move on the courts," and a massive march through Chicago's Loop. The leaflets proclaimed:

> We move with the people of the world to seize power from those who now rule. We . . . expect their pig lackeys to come down on us. We've got to be ready for that. This is a war we can't resist. We've got to actively fight. We're going to bring the war home to the mother country of imperialism. AMERIKA: THE FINAL FRONT.

From the beginning, the hundreds of "Weathermen" and "Weatherwomen" who arrived that Wednesday in Chicago behaved differently from any previous white demonstrators in America. As soon as they arrived, they organized themselves in military fashion. No one was allowed to participate in the gathering who did not belong to the Weatherman organization, not even the photographers and correspondents of the "underground" media. In the meetings themselves, briefings were given by the "Weather Bureau," the national leadership of the Weatherman. "Affinity Groups" of five or six members, who were to be the basic fighting units in the forthcoming battle with the police, were formed by local leaders. Surprised New Left members and veterans of previous confrontations with the police could not quite understand what was happening. When they tried to approach the Weatherman's members to find out, they were told:

> You can't talk about the Movement because we have to crush the Movement to build the revolution. . . . We start to build a Red Army by fighting in the streets now. We're going to knock the pig on his ass in those streets. Sure there's going to be pigs hitting people like before, but

this time there's going to be people hitting pigs. . . . The focal point is here in Chicago. We've got to show people that white kids are willing to fight on the side of black people and on the side of revolution around the world. If you're not going to fight, then you're not part of us. It's as simple as that.

Days of Rage

Violence occurred as soon as the march began. Weathermen first attacked the North Federal Savings and Loan Building, breaking its large plate-glass windows with rocks. As they moved down Clark Street they started to run, systematically smashing windows of buildings and parked cars on both sides of the street. People trying to protect their cars were beaten and left bleeding on the streets. The police, caught by surprise, did not interfere. Later, when a police line formed, the demonstrators charged into it and the line was broken.

Assessing the first evening of what became known in the history of the American protest movement as the "Days of Rage," Stephen Zicher, a Chicago assistant corporation counsel, said, "We never expected this kind of violent demonstration. There always has been a big difference between what they say and what they do." And Tom Hayden, a central figure in the protest movement of the 1960s, later said of the Weatherman action:

> We never did what the government accused us of in 1968 [at the Democratic National Convention in Chicago], but the Weathermen did it in 1969. What we did in 1968 pre-figured Weathermen; a few karate and snake dance exercises, some disruption, a lot of running in the streets, and at the end of Convention Week, a prediction that a fighting force would be created which would bring the war in Vietnam home. It remained for the government to develop this seed into a paranoid image of crazy, unruly, drug-ruined, club-carrying, Communist-inspired mobs rampaging in the Loop, and for Weathermen to fulfill the image one year later. Many Weathermen leaders were

shaped by the events of Chicago '68. When our legal protest was clubbed down they became outlaws. When our pitiful attempts at peaceful confrontation were overwhelmed, they adopted the tactic of offensive guerrilla violence.

As on other occasions, Tom Hayden was not attempting to make a detached and theoretical observation about the behavior of radicals in a time of national crisis, but in his acute and peculiar way he managed to do so. What he observed and described was the development of a crisis of legitimacy in a democracy. . . .

Soon after the "Days of Rage," the Weatherman leaders, at that time in command of the national headquarters of the Students for a Democratic Society (SDS) in Chicago, closed the offices of that organization and entrusted its massive archives to the State Historical Society of Wisconsin in Madison. Their new mood was reflected well in a headline in the Weatherman's journal, *Fire:* "DURING THE 1960S THE AMERICAN GOVERNMENT WAS ON TRIAL FOR CRIMES AGAINST THE PEOPLE OF THE WORLD. WE NOW FIND THE GOVERNMENT GUILTY AND SENTENCE IT TO DEATH ON THE STREETS."

The War Council

In a three-day "war council" in Flint, Michigan, the Weathermen came to the conclusion that they now had to become real revolutionaries. Bernardine Dohrn, the most determined leader of the organization, made it clear that "white kids," unlike their black counterparts, were not risking themselves sufficiently. Real revolution meant violence and terrorism, and this had to be the Weatherman's course. Suzan Stern, a participant at the "war council," reported on the themes that dominated the discussion:

> There was a history for us to follow. The Algerian guerrilla terrorists did play a big role in freeing Algeria from the French tyranny; [Viet Cong] terrorists, the Huks in the Philippines, the Tupamaros in Uruguay . . . the Palestinian Liberation Front. The topic was not approached lightly; it

was a deadly serious meeting. Everyone knew the implications of even *talking* about terrorism. And we were discussing what would be necessary to actually do it.

By the end of 1969 the course was set. The Weatherman, whose members already lived in very closed "collectives," went underground; it declared war on the government of the United States and announced its intention to build a Leninist vanguard and a "red army." Splitting itself into small, secret, action-oriented "affinity groups" that were subject to the hierarchical command of the "Weather Bureau," it armed itself heavily and enforced strict rules of secrecy upon its members. Through anonymous telephone calls and letters to the underground press, it claimed responsibility for otherwise unsolved cases of bombing and subversive operations. . . .

The Radicalization of the SDS

What is so intriguing about the activities of the Weatherman, from a historical and theoretical perspective, is not so much the group's antinomian delegitimation of the entire American value system in 1969 but the fact that it was the direct offspring of a student organization, the Students for a Democratic Society (SDS), which in 1962 had constituted itself as a liberal and democratic movement in order to promote the value of a "democracy of individual participation."

It is true that, in its founding manifesto, the Port Huron Statement, the SDS severely criticized the Democratic and Republican parties for being equally insensitive to the cold war, the third world, and racial discrimination at home. But the conclusion of this critique was neither a call for anti-democratic revolution nor a quest for a political system guided by a Leninist party representing the proletariat. Rather, it projected a system of "Two genuine parties, centered around issues and essential values . . . with sufficient party disagreement to dramatize major issues, yet sufficient party overlap to guarantee stable transition from administration to administration." Indeed, the SDS saw itself as a spearhead of a "New Left" concentrated on the American campus. Yet this New Left was very peaceful and nonviolent. . . .

Reflecting the impact of another student organization—the black Student Nonviolent Coordinating Committee (SNCC), an organization that fought for civil rights in the South and thereby became to the SDS a subject of great admiration and respect—the Port Huron Statement insisted on a basic commitment to a philosophy of nonviolence:

> We find violence to be abhorrent because it requires generally the transformation of the target, be it a human being or a community of people, into a depersonalized object of hate. It is imperative that the means of violence be abolished and the institutions—local, national, international—that encourage nonviolence as a condition of conflict be developed.

The SDS conceived commitment to nonviolence not as a useful tactical means to be applied temporarily against a resourceful and powerful rival but as a normative ethical principle. Violence as a political means was to be abolished because it was basically a dehumanizing pattern of behavior. Politics could do well without violence, and institutions encouraging nonviolence had to be devised. The SDS's commitment to nonviolence was thus fully congruent with its idealistic vision of the desired performance of liberal democracy as well as with its criticism of the actual performance of this system in the United States.

What happened in the seven years between the creation of the SDS and the rise of the Weatherman was the development of a process of group radicalization in which the SDS first grew into a radical mass movement and then split and shrank. The young, liberal critics of 1962 were swept up by the events of their stormy decade to an extent that neither they nor others thought possible. And in 1969 they themselves were left behind by a second generation of radicals that they had helped socialize into the politics of protest. . . .

Turning to Violence

When, in the summer of 1969, the SDS split into three factions—each adhering to a different tactical and strategic perspective—they all had one thing in common: they presented their case in militant Marxist language directed at a discredited and illegitimate political system.

The Marxization of many segments within the New Left betokened a principled delegitimation of liberal democracy. But this symbolic transformation was not used to justify illegal behavior and violence. Draft card burning, for example, was presented in the courts as a constitutional act falling within the First Amendment. The practices of confrontation with public authorities and the police, extolled by the SDS and other radical groups after 1967, also were not clear cases of illegal action. They were an extreme application of earlier tactics of direct action. If intensive violence occurred—and it did occur increasingly after 1967—it was usually not planned in advance but was a result of the interaction between impatient police and passionate demonstrators.

But the experience of low-grade violence, and the intensive use of symbols of delegitimation, have their own logic of incremental development. The tactics of confrontation were soon supplemented by the bombings of induction centers. The radical Black Panthers, who armed themselves heavily and fought the police fiercely, provided an attractive model to follow. They also produced an immense sense of guilt in the hearts of the young radicals, who believed in the same cause but did not get the same brutal treatment from the authorities. Also important was the "urban guerrilla" model provided by the Tupamaros in Uruguay. It remained for the Weatherman leaders, the second generation of the SDS who were politically socialized by the violent confrontations of the previous three years, to bring the process to its peak. This process—a psychopolitical crisis of legitimacy—was marked by a syndrome consisting of four components: (1) a political language of delegitimation of the regime, (2) rhetoric and symbols of depersonalization and dehumanization of individuals belonging to the system, (3) intended and planned violence, and (4) terrorism.

As a terror underground the Weatherman was a failure. It did not succeed, as the Red Army Faction did in West Germany, to shock an entire country. It was unable, as the Italian Red Brigades were able, to hold up a modern society at gun point. In fact, it never recruited more than four hundred members and followers, and most of the time its inexperienced leaders and recruits worried not about the revolution but about their hideouts, survival logistics, and internal group relations. Although the organization was responsible for dozens of bombings in 1970—and scored some spectacular successes, such as the explosions that took place in the Capitol, the Pentagon, and New York police headquarters—its greatest damage was self-inflicted: three leaders of the organization blew themselves up in a New York townhouse while manufacturing a bomb. Despite the Weatherman's high-revolutionary rhetoric, its young leaders never recovered from this loss; the accident greatly diminished their enthusiasm for terrorism. In their last public document, *Prairie Fire*, published in 1974, Weatherman leaders restated their revolutionary commitment to armed struggle and took credit for twenty explosions and other operations initiated over the previous years. But they admitted, at the same time, that very little had been achieved in the United States and that a long and protracted world struggle was still ahead. Nothing of significance has been heard from them since. . . .

New Left Terrorism

It is important to recognize that the conditions that promote the evolution of ideological terrorism are very different from the conditions that promote the evolution of protest and extraparliamentary politics. Most modern societies experience, at some time, some form of a crisis of confidence. . . .

The New Left terrorism that emerged in the late 1960s doubtless could not have come to existence without two critical historical conditions: the disillusionment with the war in Vietnam and the attractive models of terrorism and the urban guerrilla that developed after 1950 in the third world.

Despite the image of a widespread New Left terrorism that prevailed in the 1970s, it is important to remember that even at that time ideological terrorism was the exception rather than the rule. Most processes of delegitimation never reach the full maturation necessary for the formation of terrorism.

It is also important to recognize that radicalization is a demanding and dangerous process. . . .

Terrorism is violent, cruel, antinomian, and, most of all, deadly. People get killed or mutilated. For the radicals involved, just as for their victims, this is by far the most dangerous form of political action or warfare.

Terrorists Require Support Systems

Most of the radicals who do not achieve the stage of terrorism stay at the psychopolitical level of the crisis of confidence or at the level of the conflict of legitimacy. It is thus possible to distinguish between the avant garde of the process of delegitimation—the terrorists—and the rearguard, the great number of the other radicals who remain behind. The terrorists are usually scornful and critical of the rearguard. They see themselves as the *crème de la crème* of the revolution and perceive the others as fakes or failures. But politically and operationally they need the rearguard a great deal. No terror underground is capable of sustaining itself without a nonterrorist support system—friends and accomplices who provide information, hideouts, escape routes, and supplies. To the degree that the New Left terrorists were able to survive, they did it with the support of the less-committed rearguardists.

Ideological terrorism does not emerge from a vacuum or

from an inexplicable urge on the part of a few unstable radicals to go berserk. Rather, it is the psychopolitical product of a profound process of delegitimation that a large number of people undergo in relation to the established social and political order. Although most of the participants in this process are capable of preserving their sense of reality, a few are not. Totally consumed by their radicalism, they imagine a nonexistent "fantasy war" with the authorities and expend themselves in the struggle to win it. Ideological terrorism, in the final analysis, is the simulated revolution of the isolated few.

The U.S. Government Lacks the Moral Authority to Condemn Terrorists

TIMOTHY MCVEIGH

On April 19, 1995, Timothy McVeigh ignited a bomb that destroyed the federal building in Oklahoma City, Oklahoma, and killed 168 people, 19 of them children. McVeigh, a right-wing extremist and Gulf War veteran, held the U.S. government in contempt for purported war crimes in the Gulf and for the 1993 Bureau of Alcohol, Tobacco, and Firearms (ATF) raid of the Branch Davidian cult compound in Waco, Texas, in which more than 75 people died.

In this essay McVeigh equates the U.S. bombing of Iraq with the devastation in Oklahoma and concludes that the U.S. government is hypocritical to support the former and condemn the latter. He cites the use of nuclear weapons in Hiroshima and Nagasaki during World War II as the ultimate immorality and argues America's policy of stockpiling weapons of mass destruction while forbidding other nations from doing so is a double standard. He was sentenced to death in 1997 and executed by lethal injection in 2001.

Timothy McVeigh, "An Essay on Hypocrisy," *Media Bypass*, March 1998.

The administration has said that Iraq has no right to stockpile chemical or biological weapons ("weapons of mass destruction")—mainly because they have used them in the past.

Well, if that's the standard by which these matters are decided, then the U.S. is the nation that set the precedent. The U.S. has stockpiled these same weapons (and more) for over 40 years. The U.S. claims that this was done for deterent purposes during the "Cold War" with the Soviet Union. Why, then is it invalid for Iraq to claim the same reason (deterrence)—with respect to Iraq's (real) war with, and the continued threat of, its neighbor Iran?

The administration claims that Iraq has used these weapons in the past. We've all seen the pictures that show a Kurdish woman and child frozen in death from the use of chemical weapons. But, have you ever seen these pictures juxtaposed next to pictures from Hiroshima or Nagasaki?

I suggest that one study the histories of World War I, World War II and other "regional conflicts" that the U.S. has been involved in to familiarize themselves with the use of "weapons of mass destruction."

Remember Dresden? How about Hanoi? Tripoli? Baghdad? What about the big ones—Hiroshima and Nagasaki? (At these two locations, the U.S. killed at least 150,000 noncombatants—mostly women and children—in the blink of an eye. Thousands more took hours, days, weeks, or months to die.) If [former Iraqi leader] Saddam [Hussein] is such a demon, and people are calling for war crimes charges and trials against him and his nation, why do we not hear the same cry for blood directed at those responsible for even greater amounts of "mass destruction"—like those responsible and involved in dropping bombs on the cities mentioned above?

The truth is, the U.S. has set the standard when it comes to the stockpiling and use of weapons of mass destruction.

Hypocrisy when it comes to death of children? In Oklahoma City, it was family convenience that explained the presence of a day-care center placed between street level and the law enforcement agencies which occupied the upper floors of the building. Yet when discussion shifts to Iraq, any day-care center in a government building instantly becomes "a shield." Think about that.

(Actually, there is a difference here. The administration has admitted to knowledge of the presence of children in or near Iraqi government buildings, yet they still proceed with their plans to bomb—saying that they cannot be held responsible if children die. There is no such proof, however, that knowledge of the presence of children existed in relation to the Oklahoma City bombing.)

A Question of Morality

When considering morality and mens rea [criminal intent] in light of these facts, I ask: Who are the true barbarians?

Yet another example of this nation's blatant hypocrisy is revealed by the polls which suggest that this nation is greatly in favor of bombing Iraq. In this instance, the people of the nation approve of bombing government employees because they are "guilty by association"—they are Iraqi government employees. In regard to the bombing in Oklahoma City, however, such logic is condemned.

What motivates these seemingly contradictory positions? Do people think that government workers in Iraq are any less human than those in Oklahoma City? Do they think that Iraqis don't have families who will grieve and mourn the loss of their loved ones? In this context, do people come to believe that the killing of foreigners is somehow different than the killing of Americans?

I recently read of an arrest in New York City where possession of a mere pipe bomb was charged as possession of a "weapon of mass destruction." If a two pound pipe bomb is a "weapon of mass destruction," then what do people think that a 2,000-pound steel-encased bomb is?

I find it ironic, to say the least, that one of the aircraft that could be used to drop such a bomb on Iraq is dubbed "The Spirit of Oklahoma."

When a U.S. plane or cruise missile is used to bring destruction to a foreign people, this nation rewards the bombers with applause and praise. What a convenient way to absolve these killers of any responsibility for the destruction they leave in their wake.

Unfortunately, the morality of killing is not so superficial. The truth is, the use of a truck, a plane, or a missile for the delivery of a weapon of mass destruction does not alter the nature of the act itself. These are weapons of mass destruction—and the method of delivery matters little to those on the receiving end of such weapons.

Whether you wish to admit it or not, when you approve, morally, of the bombing of foreign targets by the U.S. military, you are approving of acts morally equivilent to the bombing in Oklahoma City. The only difference is that this nation is not going to see any foreign casualties appear on the cover of *Newsweek* magazine.

It seems ironic and hypocritical that an act viciously condemned in Oklahoma City is now a "justified" response to a problem in a foreign land. Then again, the history of United States policy over the last century, when examined fully, tends to exemplify hypocrisy.

When considering the use of weapons of mass destruction against Iraq as a means to an end, it would be wise to reflect on the words of the late U.S. Supreme Court Justice Louis Brandeis. His words are as true in the context of *Olmstead*[1] as they are when they stand alone: "Our government is the potent, the omnipresent teacher. For good or for ill, it teaches the whole people by its example."

Sincerely
Timothy J. McVeigh

1. 1928 Supreme Court case dealing with the use of electronic surveillance

Muslims Are Obligated to Kill Americans

AL QAEDA

The affiliation of terrorist groups collectively known as al Qaeda, led by Osama bin Laden, is responsible for the terrorist attacks of September 11, 2001. In the following statement, Bin Laden and four other al Qaeda members argue that U.S. terrorism against Muslims has gone unanswered. They condemn the presence of U.S. military bases on the Arabian Peninsula as an insult to God. Using text from the Koran to support its argument, al Qaeda claims that the murder of Americans, both military and civilian, is a duty to God. Al Qaeda released this statement in February 1998 under the name World Islamic Front.

"Praise be to God, who revealed the Book, controls the clouds, defeats factionalism, and says in His Book: "But when the forbidden months are past, then fight and slay the pagans wherever ye find them, seize them, beleaguer them, and lie in wait for them in every stratagem (of war)"; and peace be upon our Prophet, Muhammad Bin-'Abdallah, who said I have been sent with the sword between my hands to ensure that no one but God is worshipped, God who put my livelihood under the shadow of my spear and who inflicts humiliation and scorn on those who disobey my orders. The Arabian Peninsula has never—

---

al Qaeda, "Fatwa Urging Jihad Against Americans," February 23, 1998.

since God made it flat, created its desert, and encircled it with seas—been stormed by any forces like the crusader armies spreading in it like locusts, eating its riches and wiping out its plantations. All this is happening at a time in which nations are attacking Muslims like people fighting over a plate of food. In the light of the grave situation and the lack of support, we and you are obliged to discuss current events, and we should all agree on how to settle the matter.

No one argues today about three facts that are known to everyone; we will list them, in order to remind everyone.

Three Reasons for Jihad

First, for over seven years the United States has been occupying the lands of Islam in the holiest of places, the Arabian Peninsula, plundering its riches, dictating to its rulers, humiliating its people, terrorizing its neighbors, and turning its bases in the Peninsula into a spearhead through which to fight the neighboring Muslim peoples.

If some people have in the past argued about the fact of the occupation, all the people of the Peninsula have now acknowledged it.

The best proof of this is the Americans' continuing aggression against the Iraqi people using the Peninsula as a staging post, even though all its rulers are against their territories being used to that end, but they are helpless. Second, despite the great devastation inflicted on the Iraqi people by the crusader-Zionist alliance, and despite the huge number of those killed, which has exceeded 1 million ... despite all this, the Americans are once against trying to repeat the horrific massacres, as though they are not content with the protracted blockade imposed after the ferocious war or the fragmentation and devastation.

So here they come to annihilate what is left of this people and to humiliate their Muslim neighbors.

Third, if the Americans' aims behind these wars are religious and economic, the aim is also to serve the Jews' petty state and divert attention from its occupation of Jerusalem and murder of Muslims there.

The best proof of this is their eagerness to destroy Iraq, the strongest neighboring Arab state, and their endeavor to fragment all the states of the region such as Iraq, Saudi Arabia, Egypt, and Sudan into paper statelets and through their disunion and weakness to guarantee Israel's survival and the continuation of the brutal crusade occupation of the Peninsula.

Americans Have Declared War on God

All these crimes and sins committed by the Americans are a clear declaration of war on God, his messenger, and Muslims. And ulema [Muslim scholars] have throughout Islamic history unanimously agreed that the jihad is an individual duty if the enemy destroys the Muslim countries. This was revealed by Imam Bin-Qadamah in "Al-Mughni," Imam al-Kisa'i in "Al-Bada'i," al-Qurtubi in his interpretation, and the shaykh of al-Islam [not further identified] in his books, where he said "As for the fighting to repulse [an enemy], it is aimed at defending sanctity and religion, and it is a duty as agreed [by the ulema]. Nothing is more sacred than belief except repulsing an enemy who is attacking religion and life."

On that basis, and in compliance with God's order, we issue the following fatwa to all Muslims. The ruling to kill the Americans and their allies—civilians and military—is an individual duty for every Muslim who can do it in any country in which it is possible to do it, in order to liberate the al-Aqsa Mosque and the holy mosque [Mecca] from their grip, and in order for their armies to move out of all the lands of Islam, defeated and unable to threaten any Muslim. This is in accordance with the words of Almighty God, "and fight the pagans all together as they fight you all together," and "fight them until there is no more tumult or oppression, and there prevail justice and faith in God."

This is in addition to the words of Almighty God "And

why should ye not fight in the cause of God and of those who, being weak, are ill-treated (and oppressed)—women and children, whose cry is 'Our Lord, rescue us from this town, whose people are oppressors; and raise for us from thee one who will help!'"

We—with God's help—call on every Muslim who believes in God and wishes to be rewarded to comply with God's order to kill the Americans and plunder their money wherever and whenever they find it. We also call on Muslim ulema, leaders, youths, and soldiers to launch the raid on Satan's U.S. troops and the devil's supporters allying with them, and to displace those who are behind them so that they may learn a lesson.

Almighty God said "O ye who believe, give your response to God and His Apostle, when He calleth you to that which will give you life. And know that God cometh between a man and his heart, and that it is He to whom ye shall all be gathered."

Almighty God also says "O ye who believe, what is the matter with you, that when ye are asked to go forth in the cause of God, ye cling so heavily to the earth! Do ye prefer the life of this world to the hereafter? But little is the comfort of this life, as compared with the hereafter. Unless ye go forth, He will punish you with a grievous penalty, and put others in your place; but Him ye would not harm in the least. For God hath power over all things." Almighty God also says "So lose no heart, nor fall into despair. For ye must gain mastery if ye are true in faith."

America Must Fight Islamic Terrorists

GEORGE W. BUSH

In the weeks following September 11, 2001, after the worst terrorist attack on U.S. soil in American history, George W. Bush outlined his administration's strategies to combat Islamic terrorism in a collection of initiatives and military actions collectively known as the War on Terrorism. In this speech, delivered on September 20, Bush defines the terrorists as freedom haters, condemns states that harbor terrorists, and vows to fight violence with "patient justice."

On September the 11th, enemies of freedom committed an act of war against our country. Americans have known wars, but for the past 136 years they have been wars on foreign soil, except for one Sunday in 1941. Americans have known the casualties of war, but not at the center of a great city on a peaceful morning.

Americans have known surprise attacks, but never before on thousands of civilians. All of this was brought upon us in a single day, and night fell on a different world, a world where freedom itself is under attack.

Americans have many questions tonight. Americans are asking, "Who attacked our country?"

The evidence we have gathered all points to a collection of loosely affiliated terrorist organizations known as al Qaeda. They are some of the murderers indicted for bombing American embassies in Tanzania and Kenya and responsible for bombing the USS *Cole*.

George W. Bush, address to Congress, Washington, DC, September 20, 2001.

Who Are the Terrorists?

Al Qaeda is to terror what the Mafia is to crime. But its goal is not making money, its goal is remaking the world and imposing its radical beliefs on people everywhere.

The terrorists practice a fringe form of Islamic extremism that has been rejected by Muslim scholars and the vast majority of Muslim clerics; a fringe movement that perverts the peaceful teachings of Islam.

The terrorists' directive commands them to kill Christians and Jews, to kill all Americans and make no distinctions among military and civilians, including women and children. This group and its leader, a person named Osama bin Laden, are linked to many other organizations in different countries, including the Egyptian Islamic Jihad, the Islamic Movement of Uzbekistan.

There are thousands of these terrorists in more than 60 countries.

They are recruited from their own nations and neighborhoods and brought to camps in places like Afghanistan where they are trained in the tactics of terror. They are sent back to their homes or sent to hide in countries around the world to plot evil and destruction. The leadership of al Qaeda has great influence in Afghanistan and supports the Taliban regime in controlling most of that country. In Afghanistan we see al Qaeda's vision for the world. Afghanistan's people have been brutalized, many are starving and many have fled.

Women are not allowed to attend school. You can be jailed for owning a television. Religion can be practiced only as their leaders dictate. A man can be jailed in Afghanistan if his beard is not long enough. The United States respects the people of Afghanistan—after all, we are currently its largest source of humanitarian aid—but we condemn the Taliban regime.

It is not only repressing its own people, it is threatening people everywhere by sponsoring and sheltering and supplying terrorists.

By aiding and abetting murder, the Taliban regime is committing murder. And tonight the United States of America makes the following demands on the Taliban:

• Deliver to United States authorities all of the leaders of al Qaeda who hide in your land.

• Release all foreign nationals, including American citizens you have unjustly imprisoned.

• Protect foreign journalists, diplomats and aid workers in your country.

• Close immediately and permanently every terrorist training camp in Afghanistan. And hand over every terrorist and every person and their support structure to appropriate authorities.

• Give the United States full access to terrorist training camps, so we can make sure they are no longer operating.

These demands are not open to negotiation or discussion.

The Taliban must act and act immediately.

They will hand over the terrorists or they will share in their fate.

Islam Is Not Terrorism

I also want to speak tonight directly to Muslims throughout the world. We respect your faith. It's practiced freely by many millions of Americans and by millions more in countries that America counts as friends. Its teachings are good and peaceful, and those who commit evil in the name of Allah blaspheme the name of Allah.

The terrorists are traitors to their own faith, trying, in effect, to hijack Islam itself.

The enemy of America is not our many Muslim friends. It is not our many Arab friends. Our enemy is a radical network of terrorists and every government that supports them.

Our war on terror begins with al Qaeda, but it does not end there.

It will not end until every terrorist group of global reach has been found, stopped and defeated.

Terrorists Hate Freedom

Americans are asking "Why do they hate us?"

They hate what they see right here in this chamber: a democratically elected government. Their leaders are self-appointed. They hate our freedoms: our freedom of religion, our freedom of speech, our freedom to vote and assemble and disagree with each other.

They want to overthrow existing governments in many Muslim countries such as Egypt, Saudi Arabia and Jordan. They want to drive Israel out of the Middle East. They want to drive Christians and Jews out of vast regions of Asia and Africa.

These terrorists kill not merely to end lives, but to disrupt and end a way of life. With every atrocity, they hope that America grows fearful, retreating from the world and forsaking our friends. They stand against us because we stand in their way.

We're not deceived by their pretenses to piety.

We have seen their kind before. They're the heirs of all the murderous ideologies of the 20th century. By sacrificing human life to serve their radical visions, by abandoning every value except the will to power, they follow in the path of fascism, Nazism and totalitarianism. And they will follow that path all the way to where it ends in history's unmarked grave of discarded lies. Americans are asking, "How will we fight and win this war?"

Strategies to Combat Terror

We will direct every resource at our command—every means of diplomacy, every tool of intelligence, every instrument of law enforcement, every financial influence, and every necessary weapon of war—to the destruction and to the defeat of the global terror network.

Now, this war will not be like the war against Iraq a decade ago, with a decisive liberation of territory and a swift conclusion. It will not look like the air war above Kosovo two years ago, where no ground troops were used

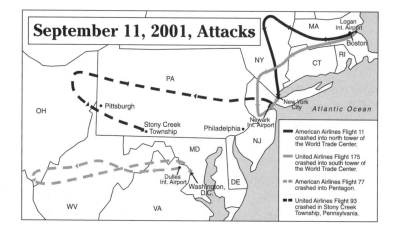

September 11, 2001, Attacks

MA — Logan Int. Airport
Boston
NY
CT
RI
PA
OH
Pittsburgh
New York City — Atlantic Ocean
Stony Creek Township
Philadelphia
Newark Int. Airport
NJ
MD
Dulles Int. Airport
Washington, D.C.
DE
WV
VA

- American Airlines Flight 11 crashed into north tower of the World Trade Center.
- United Airlines Flight 175 crashed into south tower of the World Trade Center.
- American Airlines Flight 77 crashed into Pentagon.
- United Airlines Flight 93 crashed in Stony Creek Township, Pennsylvania.

and not a single American was lost in combat.

Our response involves far more than instant retaliation and isolated strikes. Americans should not expect one battle, but a lengthy campaign unlike any other we have ever seen. It may include dramatic strikes visible on TV and covert operations secret even in success.

We will starve terrorists of funding, turn them one against another, drive them from place to place until there is no refuge or no rest.

And we will pursue nations that provide aid or safe haven to terrorism. Every nation in every region now has a decision to make: Either you are with us or you are with the terrorists.

From this day forward, any nation that continues to harbor or support terrorism will be regarded by the United States as a hostile regime. Our nation has been put on notice, we're not immune from attack. We will take defensive measures against terrorism to protect Americans. Today, dozens of federal departments and agencies, as well as state and local governments, have responsibilities affecting homeland security.

These efforts must be coordinated at the highest level. So tonight, I announce the creation of a Cabinet-level position reporting directly to me, the Office of Homeland Security. And tonight, I also announce a distinguished American to lead this effort, to strengthen American security: a military veteran, an effective governor, a true patriot, a trusted friend, Pennsylvania's Tom Ridge.

He will lead, oversee and coordinate a comprehensive national strategy to safeguard our country against terrorism and respond to any attacks that may come. These measures are essential. The only way to defeat terrorism as a threat to our way of life is to stop it, eliminate it and destroy it where it grows.

Many will be involved in this effort, from FBI agents, to intelligence operatives, to the reservists we have called to active duty. All deserve our thanks, and all have our prayers. And tonight a few miles from the damaged Pentagon, I have a message for our military: Be ready. I have called the armed forces to alert, and there is a reason.

The hour is coming when America will act, and you will make us proud.

The Civilized World Opposes Terrorism

This is not, however, just America's fight. And what is at stake is not just America's freedom. This is the world's fight. This is civilization's fight. This is the fight of all who believe in progress and pluralism, tolerance and freedom.

We ask every nation to join us.

We will ask and we will need the help of police forces, intelligence service and banking systems around the world. The United States is grateful that many nations and many international organizations have already responded with sympathy and with support—nations from Latin America to Asia to Africa to Europe to the Islamic world.

Perhaps the NATO charter reflects best the attitude of the world: An attack on one is an attack on all. The civilized world is rallying to America's side.

They understand that if this terror goes unpunished, their own cities, their own citizens may be next. Terror unanswered can not only bring down buildings, it can threaten the stability of legitimate governments.

And you know what? We're not going to allow it.

Americans are asking, "What is expected of us?"

I ask you to live your lives and hug your children. I know many citizens have fears tonight, and I ask you to be calm and resolute, even in the face of a continuing threat.

I ask you to uphold the values of America and remember why so many have come here.

We're in a fight for our principles, and our first responsibility is to live by them. No one should be singled out for unfair treatment or unkind words because of their ethnic background or religious faith.

I ask you to continue to support the victims of this tragedy with your contributions. Those who want to give can go to a central source of information, Libertyunites.org, to find the names of groups providing direct help in New York, Pennsylvania and Virginia. The thousands of FBI agents who are now at work in this investigation may need your cooperation, and I ask you to give it. I ask for your patience with the delays and inconveniences that may accompany tighter security and for your patience in what will be a long struggle.

I ask your continued participation and confidence in the American economy. Terrorists attacked a symbol of American prosperity; they did not touch its source.

America is successful because of the hard work and creativity and enterprise of our people. These were the true strengths of our economy before September 11, and they are our strengths today.

And finally, please continue praying for the victims of terror and their families, for those in uniform and for our great country. Prayer has comforted us in sorrow and will help strengthen us for the journey ahead. Tonight I thank my fellow Americans for what you have already done and for what you will do.

And ladies and gentlemen of the Congress, I thank you, their representatives, for what you have already done and for what we will do together.

An Age of Terror

Tonight we face new and sudden national challenges. We will come together to improve air safety, to dramatically expand the number of air marshals on domestic flights and take new measures to prevent hijacking.

We will come together to promote stability and keep our airlines flying with direct assistance during this emergency.

We will come together to give law enforcement the additional tools it needs to track down terror here at home.

We will come together to strengthen our intelligence capabilities to know the plans of terrorists before they act and to find them before they strike.

We will come together to take active steps that strengthen America's economy and put our people back to work.

Tonight, we welcome two leaders who embody the extraordinary spirit of all New Yorkers, Governor George Pataki and Mayor Rudolph Giuliani.

As a symbol of America's resolve, my administration will work with Congress and these two leaders to show the world that we will rebuild New York City.

After all that has just passed, all the lives taken and all the possibilities and hopes that died with them, it is natural to wonder if America's future is one of fear.

Some speak of an age of terror. I know there are struggles ahead and dangers to face. But this country will define our times, not be defined by them.

As long as the United States of America is determined and strong, this will not be an age of terror. This will be an age of liberty here and across the world.

Great harm has been done to us. We have suffered great loss. And in our grief and anger we have found our mission and our moment.

Freedom and fear are at war. The advance of human freedom, the great achievement of our time and the great hope of every time, now depends on us.

Our nation, this generation, will lift the dark threat of violence from our people and our future. We will rally the world to this cause by our efforts, by our courage. We will not tire, we will not falter and we will not fail.

It is my hope that in the months and years ahead life will return almost to normal. We'll go back to our lives and routines and that is good.

Even grief recedes with time and grace.

But our resolve must not pass. Each of us will remember what happened that day and to whom it happened. We will remember the moment the news came, where we were and what we were doing.

Some will remember an image of a fire or story or rescue. Some will carry memories of a face and a voice gone forever.

And I will carry this. It is the police shield of a man named George Howard who died at the World Trade Center trying to save others.

It was given to me by his mom, Arlene, as a proud memorial to her son. It is my reminder of lives that ended and a task that does not end.

I will not forget the wound to our country and those who inflicted it. I will not yield, I will not rest, I will not relent in waging this struggle for freedom and security for the American people. The course of this conflict is not known, yet its outcome is certain. Freedom and fear, justice and cruelty, have always been at war, and we know that God is not neutral between them.

Fellow citizens, we'll meet violence with patient justice, assured of the rightness of our cause and confident of the victories to come.

In all that lies before us, may God grant us wisdom and may He watch over the United States of America.

Thank you.

America Is a Terrorist State

NOAM CHOMSKY

Noam Chomsky is an award-winning professor of linguistics who has written extensively on U.S. foreign policy and international affairs. In this piece Chomsky argues that the American people are either blind to or ignorant of the terror perpetrated by the U.S. government. Among other incidents, he cites the August 1998 bombing of the Al-Shifa medical plant in Sudan, a crucial source of human and veterinary medicine. Repercussions from this attack were proportionate in magnitude to those of the September 11 terrorist attacks on America, he argues. He also asserts that intelligence failures, such as missed opportunities to glean information regarding the whereabouts of Osama bin Laden, only compound America's tragic mishandling of foreign policy.

The most obvious example [of American terrorism], though far from the most extreme case, is Nicaragua. It is the most obvious because it is uncontroversial, at least to people who have even the faintest concern for international law. It is worth remembering—particularly since it has been so uniformly suppressed—that the U.S. is the only country that was condemned for international terrorism by the World Court and that rejected a Security Council resolution calling on states to observe international law.

The United States continues international terrorism. There are also what in comparison are minor examples.

Everybody here was quite properly outraged by the Oklahoma City bombing, and for a couple of days the headlines read, "Oklahoma City Looks Like Beirut." I didn't see anybody point out that Beirut also looks like Beirut, and part of the reason is that the Reagan administration had set off a terrorist bombing there in 1985 that was very much like Oklahoma City, a truck bombing outside a mosque timed to kill the maximum number of people as they left. It killed 80 and wounded 250, mostly women and children, according to a report in the *Washington Post* 3 years later. The terrorist bombing was aimed at a Muslim cleric whom they didn't like and whom they missed. It was not very secret. I don't know what name you give to the policies that are a leading factor in the death of maybe a million civilians in Iraq and maybe a half a million children, which is the price the Secretary of State says we're willing to pay. Is there a name for that? Supporting Israeli atrocities is another one.

Supporting Turkey's crushing of its own Kurdish population, for which the Clinton administration gave the decisive support, 80 percent of the arms, escalating as atrocities increased, is another. And that was a truly massive atrocity, one of the worst campaigns of ethnic cleansing and destruction in the 1990s, scarcely known because of the primary U.S. responsibility—and when impolitely brought up, dismissed as a minor "flaw" in our general dedication to "ending inhumanity" everywhere.

Tragedy at Al-Shifa

Or take the destruction of the Al-Shifa pharmaceutical plant in Sudan, one little footnote in the record of state terror, quickly forgotten. What would the reaction have been if the bin Laden network had blown up half the pharmaceutical supplies in the U.S. and the facilities for replenishing them? We can imagine, though the comparison is unfair: the consequences are vastly more severe in Sudan. That aside, if the U.S. or Israel or England were to be the target of such an atrocity, what would the reaction be? In this case we say, "Oh, well, too bad, minor mistake, let's go on to the next topic, let the victims rot." Other people in the world don't react like that. When bin Laden brings up that bombing, he strikes a resonant chord, even among those who despise and fear him; and the same, unfortunately, is true of much of the rest of his rhetoric.

Though it is merely a footnote, the Sudan case is nonetheless highly instructive. One interesting aspect is the reaction when someone dares to mention it. I have in the past, and did so again in response to queries from journalists shortly after the 9-11 atrocities [the September 11, 2001, terrorist attacks on America]. I mentioned that the toll of the "horrendous crime" of 9-11, committed with "wickedness and awesome cruelty" (quoting Robert Fisk), may be comparable to the consequences of [Bill] Clinton's bombing of the Al-Shifa plant in August 1998. That plausible conclusion elicited an extraordinary reaction, filling many web sites and journals with feverish and fanciful condemnations, which I'll ignore. The only important aspect is that that single sentence—which, on a closer look, appears to be an understatement—was regarded by some commentators as utterly scandalous. It is difficult to avoid the conclusion that at some deep level, however they may deny it to themselves, they regard our crimes against the weak to be as normal as the air we breathe. Our crimes, for which we are responsible: as taxpayers, for failing to provide massive reparations, for granting refuge and immunity to the perpetrators, and for allowing the terrible facts to be sunk deep in the memory hole. All of this is of great significance, as it has been in the past.

About the consequences of the destruction of the Al-Shifa plant, we have only estimates. Sudan sought a UN inquiry into the justifications for the bombing, but even that was blocked by Washington, and few seem to have tried to investigate beyond. But we surely should. Perhaps we should begin by recalling some virtual truisms, at least among those with a minimal concern for human rights.

When we estimate the human toll of a crime, we count not only those who were literally murdered on the spot but those who died as a result. That is the course we adopt reflexively, and properly, when we consider the crimes of official enemies—Stalin, Hitler, and Mao, to mention the most extreme cases. Here, we do not consider the crime to be mitigated by the fact that it was not intended but was a reflection of institutional and ideological structures: the Chinese famine of 1958–1961, to take an extreme case, is not dismissed on grounds that it was a "mistake" and that Mao did not "intend" to kill tens of millions of people. Nor is it mitigated by speculations about his personal reasons for the orders that led to the famine. Similarly, we would dismiss with contempt the charge that condemnation of Hitler's crimes in Eastern Europe overlooks Stalin's crimes. If we are even pretending to be serious, we apply the same standards to ourselves, always. In this case, we count the number who died as a consequence of the crime, not just those killed in Khartoum by cruise missiles; and we do not consider the crime to be mitigated by the fact that it reflects the normal functioning of policymaking and ideological institutions—as it did, even if there is some validity to the (to my mind, dubious) speculations about Clinton's personal problems, which are irrelevant to this question anyway, for the reasons that everyone takes for granted when considering the crimes of official enemies. . . .

According to credible analyses readily available to us . . . proportional to population, the destruction of Al-Shifa is as if the bin Laden network, in a single attack on the U.S., caused "hundreds of thousands of people—many of them children—to suffer and die from easily treatable diseases," though the analogy, as noted, is unfair. Sudan is "one of the least developed areas in the world. Its harsh climate, scattered populations, health hazards and crumbling infrastructure combine to make life for many Sudanese a struggle for survival"; a country with endemic malaria, tuberculosis, and many other diseases, where "periodic outbreaks of meningitis or cholera are not un-common," so affordable medicines are a dire necessity (Jonathan Belke and Kamal El-Faki, technical reports from the field for the Near East Foundation). It is, furthermore, a country with limited arable land, a chronic shortage of potable water, a huge death rate, little industry, an unser-viceable debt, wracked with AIDS, devastated by a vicious and destructive internal war, and under severe sanctions. What is happening within is largely speculation, including Belke's (quite plausible) estimate that within a year tens of thousands had already "suffered and died" as the result of the destruction of the major facilities for producing af-fordable drugs and veterinary medicines. . . .

Intelligence Failures Compound Tragedy

The bombing also carried severe costs for the people of the United States, as became glaringly evident on September 11, or should have. It seems to me remarkable that this has not been brought up prominently (if at all), in the ex-tensive discussion of intelligence failures that lie behind the 9-11 atrocities.

Just before the 1998 missile strike, Sudan detained two men suspected of bombing the American embassies in East Africa, notifying Washington, U.S. officials confirmed. But the U.S. rejected Sudan's offer of cooperation, and after the mis-sile attack, Sudan "angrily released" the suspects (James Risen, *New York Times*, July 30, 1999); they have since been identified as bin Laden operatives. Recently leaked FBI memos add another reason why Sudan "angrily released" the suspects. The memos reveal that the FBI wanted them extradited, but the State Department refused. One "senior CIA source" now describes this and other rejections of Su-danese offers of cooperation as "the worst single intelligence failure in this whole terrible business" of September 11. "It is the key to the whole thing right now" because of the vo-luminous evidence on bin Laden that Sudan offered to pro-duce, offers that were repeatedly rebuffed because of the administration's "irrational hatred" of Sudan, the senior CIA source reports. Included in Sudan's rejected offers was "a vast intelligence database on Osama bin Laden and more than 200 leading members of his al-Qaeda terrorist network in the years leading up to the 11 September attacks." Washington was "offered thick files, with photographs and detailed biographies of many of his principal cadres, and vital information about al-Qaeda's financial interests in many parts of the globe," but refused to accept the information, out of "irrational hatred" of the target of its missile attack. "It is reasonable to say that had we had this data we may have had a better chance of preventing the attacks" of September 11, the same senior CIA source concludes (David Rose, *Observer*, September 30, reporting an *Observer* investigation).

Sudanese Victims and Reaction in the West

One can scarcely try to estimate the toll of the Sudan bombing, even apart from the probable tens of thousands of immediate Sudanese victims. The complete toll is attributable to the single act of terror—at least, if we have the honesty to adopt the standards we properly apply to official enemies. The reaction in the West tells us a lot about ourselves, if we agree to adopt another moral truism: look into the mirror.

Or to return to "our little region over here which never has bothered anybody," as Henry Stimson called the Western hemisphere, take Cuba. After many years of terror beginning in late 1959, including very serious atrocities, Cuba should have the right to resort to violence against the U.S. according to U.S. doctrine that is scarcely questioned. It is, unfortunately, all too easy to continue, not only with regard to the U.S. but also other terrorist states.

THE
HISTORY
OF
ISSUES

CHAPTER 5

Debating the Definition of Terrorism

The Nature and Causes of International Terrorism

UNITED NATIONS

On November 2, 1972, a UN committee met to discuss actions it could take to battle international terrorism. This marked the first occasion that the United Nations attempted to set the parameters for a working definition of international terrorism. The following selection is excerpted from the committee's report. The United Nations ascribes a broad set of characteristics to terrorism, such as conspicuous violence, the endangerment of innocents, and political or apolitical motivation, yet fails to reach a consensus on the nature and scope of the problem. The United Nations concludes that much terrorism is the result of "misery, frustration, grievance and despair."

The elaboration of a precise definition of international terrorism is a task which may eventually devolve on the General Assembly or on some other body. For the purpose, however, of preparing a report dealing with the origins and underlying causes of international terrorism, it is necessary to formulate, at least in broad outline, a concept of the area to be dealt with.

The present agenda item deals only with *international* ter-

United Nations, "The Origins and Fundamental Causes of International Terrorism," *Report of the Ad Hoc Committee on International Terrorism*, 1973.

rorism. It thus excludes activities that are the internal affairs of individual States. The acts of Governments within their own territories in respect of their own citizens have already been extensively dealt with in the work of the United Nations, in particular in that on human rights. To come within the scope of the subject, the interests of more than one State must be involved, as, for example, when the perpetrator or the victim is a foreigner in the country where the act is done, or the perpetrator has fled to another country.

The ordinary meaning of the word *terrorism* has undergone an evolution since it first came into use at the end of the eighteenth century, and has been differently interpreted according to the different types of acts which were uppermost at the time in the minds of those discussing the subject. While at first it applied mainly to those acts and policies of Governments which were designed to spread terror among a population for the purpose of ensuring its submission to and conformity with the will of those Governments, it now seems to be mainly applied to actions by individuals, or groups of individuals.

Terrorism, as shown by the derivation of the word, involves the infliction of terror. This is not always done to the immediate victims, who may be destroyed without warning, but the act must be such as to spread terror or alarm among a given population, or among broad groups of people. The act is necessarily a conspicuously violent one, which is often intended to focus public attention and to coerce a State into a particular action. One of the most effective means towards that aim is to endanger, threaten or take innocent human lives and to jeopardize fundamental freedoms.

At various times during the previous work on the subject at the international level, discussion was restricted to terrorist acts with political motives. Yet it is now found that quite similar acts, spreading similar terror or alarm among the population, are done for ordinary criminal motives, such as extortion of large sums. It seems difficult to delimit a legal topic on the basis of motives, which often lie hidden deep in the minds of men. Both political and non-political acts constitute current problems. From the standpoint of the effect on the innocent, there is no reason to limit international discussion to terrorist acts with political aims, while leaving aside very similar acts with ordinary criminal aims.

The subject of international terrorism has, as the Secretary-General has already emphasized, nothing to do with the question of when the use of force is legitimate in international life. On that question the provisions of the Charter, general international law, and the declarations and resolutions of the United Nations organs, in particular those of the General Assembly relating to national liberation movements, are not and cannot be affected. But even when the use of force is legally and morally justified, there are some means, as in every form of human conflict, which must not be used; the legitimacy of a cause does not in itself legitimize the use of certain forms of violence, especially against the innocent. This has long been recognized even in the customary law of war.

International terrorism has also a different character from revolutionary mass movements, which are directly aimed at, and capable of, effecting radical changes in society, involving changes of conduct and attitude on the part of large numbers of people. The terrorist act, on the other hand, even if its main purpose is to draw attention to a political cause or situation, has as its immediate aim something comparatively limited, although important, such as the acquisition of funds, the liberation of prisoners, the spread of general terror, the demonstration of the impotence of Government authorities, or the provocation of ill-judged measures of repression which will alienate public opinion. Thus the terrorist act usually lacks any immediate possibility of achieving its proclaimed ultimate purpose.

Causes of Terrorism

The causation of human action has as yet been most incompletely explained by modern psychology, genetics, sociology and related disciplines. In particular, in the field of use of violence by individuals, barely a beginning has been made in identifying underlying conditions and correlating them with particular acts; and such correlations, even if established, do not explain why only a few at most of those exposed to those conditions become criminals. The discussion of the causes of terrorism is thus apt to give rise to disagreement. This is all the more so since certain terrorist acts may be viewed by some as serious crimes, while to others they are acts of patriotism or heroism. The following remarks are made in compliance with the request of the Sixth Committee, but cannot aspire to be either complete or universally convincing, nor has any attempt been made to deal with any specific historical or current situations with which terrorism has been associated.

Men is one of the few species that frequently uses violence against its own kind. He has done so since the dawn of history. In the past, periods in which violence has been especially conspicuous have been those of rapid social change. During the years of the existence of the United Nations, when in most parts of the world, and in both the developed and the developing countries, the patterns of society are changing with almost unprecedented speed, violence has been frequent.

The interlinked growth of technology and growth of population have tended to create new hopes, expectations and needs in many social groups. These new attitudes mark a departure from the resignation and passivity with which most men in the past accepted the ills of life. The United Nations Charter is the voice of the aspirations of mankind when it contemplates the establishment of a world in which aggression and the threat or use of force in international relations would be effectively outlawed, friendly relations would exist among nations on the basis of respect for the principles of equal rights and self-determination of peoples, international disputes would be settled justly by peaceful means, and international co-operation would solve international economic and social problems and promote respect for human rights and fundamental freedoms for all.

The period of the existence of the United Nations, however, has shown very incomplete and uneven progress towards these goals. While major wars involving the great Powers have not occurred, force has often been resorted to, and has inflicted suffering and exile upon peoples. While progress has been made against colonialism and racism, those evils have not yet been completely eliminated. Even where political independence has been established, in many cases much remains to be done in assisting the populations to attain the minimum level necessary for decent conditions of life. Few advances have been made towards the peaceful settlement of some major international disputes, which are too often left to fester and poison international relations. Among groups where economic and social progress has been relatively slow, conditions have been unfavourable to the exercise of and the respect for human rights and fundamental freedoms.

The lack or slowness of advance towards these goals has contributed toward the "misery, frustration, grievance and despair" which, while not themselves causes of terrorism, are psychological conditions or states of being which sometimes lead, directly or indirectly, to the commission of acts of violence. While in the United Nations context it is perhaps appropriate to give special attention to the international factors that contribute to violence, there are also many situations in individual nations which may give rise to the grievance of a particular group or person, leading to acts having international repercussions. Purely personal circumstances can also often have the same result. There are also cases in which there is no genuine grievance at all, and a violent crime affecting more than one country seems to have been committed from mere cupidity, or a desire to escape criminal prosecution. The General Assembly, however, in stressing "misery, frustration, grievance and dispair," seems to have singled out for special attention those situations which have the common characteristic of calling for redress.

Different Forms of International Terror

Why is it that the violence resulting from these circumstances takes with increasing frequency the form of international terrorism, threatening, endangering or killing innocent victims? As the peoples of the world grow more interdependent the solution of many problems no longer hangs on any local ruler or government, but on actions and decisions taken thousands of miles away. Men think their ills have been produced by some vast impersonal force, which is deaf to their pleas for justice or impotent to find solutions, rather than by other men, striving for similar although opposed ends and bound to them by the claims of a common humanity. Modern communications and the growth of the public information media have transformed local incidents into world events, especially when the incidents have an international character. A terrorist act focuses world attention upon the terrorist and upon any cause he may claim to represent. In these circumstances, some such acts—which, as has already been said, cannot possibly by themselves effect radical social changes—are really acts of communication. They are intended to show the world that the determination and devotion of the terrorists are sufficient to compensate in the long run for their apparent inferiority in strength; that their cause is more holy to them than life itself, must be taken seriously, and is worthy of support; and that neither their foe nor the world at large is able to prevent their success in their purpose, or ensure punishment of their deeds and those of their associates.

Other such acts, however, seem to be more the result of blind fanaticism, or of the adoption of an extremist ideology which subordinates morality and all other human values to a single aim. In either case, the result is the same; modern life and modern weapons bring more and more strangers and foreigners within the reach of the terrorist, and he uses them as instruments for his purpose. As violence breeds violence, so terrorism begets counter-terrorism, which in turn leads to more terrorism in an ever-increasing spiral.

The modern aircraft—which is perhaps the most vulnerable of all the high and complex developments of technology, which contains assemblages of people from many countries, and which if brought under the terrorists' control, offers a speedy and safe means of reaching a distant asylum abroad—is often a factor in modern forms of international terrorism. The many problems of protecting aircraft without destroying the speed and convenience of air travel, or imposing unacceptable procedures upon air travellers, have not yet been completely solved.

It thus appears that the "misery, frustration, grievance and despair" which lead to terrorism have many roots in international and national political, economic and social situations affecting the terrorist, as well as in his personal circumstances. The precise chain of causation of particular acts cannot be traced with scientific exactitude. Nevertheless, the General Assembly may wish to identify types of situations which, if a remedy could be found to bring them more into accord with justice, will cease to contribute to the spreading terrorism which has shocked the world.

Myths About Terrorism

WALTER LAQUEUR

The following selection is excerpted from historian Walter Laqueur's landmark book The Age of Terrorism, *which is a revision of his 1977 work* Terrorism. *The author argues that Western governments grant more attention to terrorism that it deserves considering the small proportion of people it affects. He argues that scholarly efforts to define terrorism are unproductive and that common myths about terrorism are too often taken as facts. These myths include the belief that terrorism is a new and urgent problem, that it can be a moral response to oppression and injustice, and that it can happen anywhere. He asserts that the true danger lies not in terrorism itself but in the possibility that terrorist actions could trigger full-scale war.*

T errorism, one of the most widely discussed issues of our time, remains one of the least understood. Its recent manifestations have been described in countless books, monographs, articles, plays, novels and films at all possible levels of sophistication; terrorism has fascinated the metaphysicians as much as the popular novelists. . . .

No one is likely to deny that the number of victims and the amount of suffering caused by tyrannical and aggressive governments throughout history has been infinitely greater than that caused by small groups of rebels. A Hitler or a Stalin have killed in one year more people than all terrorists throughout recorded history. Violence and oppression have been an 'integral component' not just during the last few years, not just of the 'modern state', but throughout all recorded history. Massacres and arbitrary rule have figured prominently in primitive society and primitive religion, from the catacombs of the victims of ancient Mexico to the days of the Inquisition, from the days of the tyrannies to the absolutist rule in early modern history. The idea of freedom and human rights has made significant progress only during the last two centuries. To write the history of oppression and persecution is to write the history of mankind.

Differences Between State Oppression and Terrorism

But there are basic differences in motive, function and effect between oppression by the state (or society, or religion) and political terrorism. To equate them, to obliterate these differences, is to spread confusion and to impede the understanding of both. . . .

Terrorism is a violent phenomenon and it is probably no mere coincidence that it should give rise to violent emotions, such as anger, irritation and aggression, and that this should cloud judgement. Nor is the confusion surrounding it all new. Terrorism has long exercised a great fascination, especially at a safe distance, and has always engendered greatly divergent opinions and images. The fascination it exerts (Shelley's[1] 'tempestuous loveliness of terror'), and the difficulty of interpreting it, have the same roots; it has an unexpected, shocking and outrageous character. War, even civil war, is predictable in many ways. It occurs in the light of day and there is no mystery about the identity of the participants. Even in civil war there are certain rules, whereas the characteristic features of terrorism are anonymity and the violation of established norms. The popular image of the terrorist some ninety years ago was that of a bomb-

1. English poet Percy B. Shelley

throwing, alien anarchist, dishevelled with a black beard and a satanic (or idiotic) smile, a fanatic who was immoral, sinister and ridiculous at the same time. Dostoevski[2] and Conrad[3] provided more sophisticated but essentially similar descriptions. His present-day image has been streamlined but not necessarily improved; it certainly has not been explained by political scientists or psychiatrists called in for rapid consultation. Perhaps it is unfair to blame them, for there are so many different kinds of terrorists that generalizations are almost bound to be misleading. . . .

The Character of Terrorism

The interpretation of terrorism is difficult for yet other reasons. Even over the last century, the character of terrorism has changed greatly. This goes not only for its methods, but also for the aims of the struggle, and the character of the people that were and are involved in it. Only two generations divide Sofia Perovskaya[4] and Emma Goldman[5] from Ulrike Meinhor[6] and Patty Hearst[7] (not to mention Carlos[8] and the various Abu Nidals[9]) yet morally and intellectually the distance between them is to be measured in light years. The other difficulty is equally fundamental. Unlike Marxism, terrorism is not an ideology but an insurrectional strategy that can be used by people of very different political convictions. For this reason, simplistic explanations should be rejected *tout court.* Contemporary terrorism is not the child of Marxism-Leninism or Muslim fundamentalism, even though regimes of these creeds have made notable contributions to the spread of terrorism. Much of the prevailing confusion on the subject of terrorism would not have occurred if those delivering sweeping statements did not suffer from partial blindness. In their anger (or enthu-

2. Russian author Fyodor Dostoevski   3. Polish novelist Joseph Conrad   4. revolutionary wife of terrorist Andrei Zhelyabov, participant in bomb attacks against the Russian government   5. anarchist organizer and orator   6. German leftist terrorist   7. kidnapped newspaper heiress   8. convicted terrorist   9. Muslim extremist terrorists

siasm) they have focused on one specific kind of terrorism, ignoring the fact that there are also other kinds which do not fit their preconceptions. Yet terrorism is not only a technique. Those practising it today have certain basic beliefs in common. They may belong to the left or the right; they may be nationalists or, very rarely, internationalists, but in some essential respects their mental make-up is often similar. They are closer to each other than they know, or would like to admit to themselves. And as the technology of terrorism can be mastered by people of all creeds, so does its basic philosophy transcend the traditional dividing lines between political doctrines. It is truly all-purpose and value-free. . . .

My study of terrorism initially grew out of dissatisfaction with many current attempts to explain and interpret political terrorism, on both the popular and the academic levels. Writing in 1976, I listed a number of widespread but mistaken beliefs concerning the main features of contemporary terrorism. Writing ten years later, this list must be expanded.

Myths About Terrorism

Among these erroneous beliefs, the following should be singled out:

1. Terrorism is a new and unprecedented phenomenon. For this reason, its antecedents (if any) are of little interest. But whereas modern technology has, of course, made a great difference as far as the character of terrorist operations are concerned, the basic issues concerning terrorism—political, moral, legal—are anything but new.

2. Terrorism is one of the most important and dangerous problems facing mankind today and it should figure uppermost on our agenda. . . . There has not been so far a single case of a society dragged down to destruction as a result of terrorism, nor has there been inexorable growth. More Americans were killed in terrorist attacks in 1974 (forty-two) than in 1984 (eleven), and the number of ter-

rorist bombings has been fairly constant ever since statistics were first compiled some twenty years ago. The killing of even a single human being—let alone mass murder—is a tragedy and a crime that should be punished. The attitude towards terrorism should certainly not be one of benign neglect. But the figures show that the medical metaphor is quite misleading with regard to both the extent of the disease and its likely course.

3. The moralists claim that terrorism is the natural response to injustice, oppression and persecution. Terrorism has indeed developed in answer to repression, more often in the nineteenth century than in the twentieth. In our time the record shows that the more severe the repression, the less terrorism occurs. This is an uncomfortable and shocking fact, and many therefore refuse to accept it. Even in democratic countries the argument frequently does not hold water; terrorism in Spain gathered strength only after [Francisco] Franco died, while the terrorist upswing in West Germany and Turkey took place under social democratic or left-of-centre governments. The same is true of Colombia and Peru. More examples could easily be adduced.

4. The corollary of the moralist (terrorism-as-a-punishment) thesis is that the only known means of reducing the likelihood of terrorism is a reduction of the grievances, stresses and frustrations underlying it. There is no denying the existence of grievances, for instance on the part of national minorities. In some instances, these grievances can be put right, but frequently they cannot. In an ideal world each group of people claiming the right to full independence and statehood should receive it. In the real world, given the lack of national homogeneity, this may not be possible. An Armenian state on Turkish territory is not a practical possibility, and a Sikh state in the Punjab would not be viable, quite apart from the fact that the great majority of Sikhs do not even want it. An independent Euzkadi or Corsica would be against the wishes of the majority of the population, which is neither Basque nor Corsican.

These are but a few examples. Nor is it certain that the establishment of new independent states would put an end to terrorism; on the contrary, a violent struggle for power between various terrorist groups might intensify, between 'moderates', who want to proceed with the business of statehood, and 'radicals' claiming that what has been achieved is only a beginning, and that the borders of the new state should be expanded.

5. But if the moralists are wrong, does it not follow that, as the relativists argue, 'one-man's terrorist is another man's freedom fighter'? Of all the observations on terrorism this is surely one of the tritest. There is no unanimity on any subject under the sun, and it is perfectly true that terrorists do have well-wishers. But such support does not tell us anything about the justice of their cause; in 1941 Hitler and Mussolini had many fanatical followers. Does it follow that they fought for a just cause?

6. Yet another argument claims that terrorists are fanatical believers driven to despair by intolerable conditions. Ideas cannot be suppressed by imprisonment and executions, and for this reason terrorism will persist unless conditions change. But the evidence does not bear this out. The terrorist reservoir is not unlimited. If enough terrorists are killed (as in Khomeini's Iran) or arrested (as in Turkey, Italy and other countries), terrorism ceases to be an effective force. Some terroristic activity may continue, but it is no more than a minor nuisance.

7. Terrorists are poor and their inspiration is deeply ideological. This was more correct fifty or a hundred years ago than it is today. Terrorists belonging to international, state-sponsored networks, linked with oil producers and narco-terrorism, are no longer poor—indeed they cannot afford to be poor given the rising cost of terrorist warfare. In the old days, a dagger was sufficient, while today millions of dollars are needed for financing a terrorist infrastructure. Only the terrorist proletariat is poor. Ideology does play a role, because without ideological motivation

few people would be willing to risk their lives. But ideology alone does not explain terrorism. If it were different, then [ruler of Libya Muammar] Qadhafi would not have to advertise for terrorists in newspapers from Morocco to India.

8. Terrorism is essentially a Middle Eastern problem, and most of the victims of terrorism are American. Make peace between Israel and the Arabs, give the Palestinians a homeland and terrorism will cease—or at least very much decline. Peace in the Middle East is highly desirable for a variety of reasons, and a great many people have tried to bring it about, unfortunately without much success. But since there are at present [1987] many more anti-American terrorist incidents in Latin America (369) and Western Europe (458) than in the Middle East (84), there is no good reason to suppose that peace between the Arabs and Israel would have a significant effect on anti-American terrorism.

9. State-sponsored terrorism presents a new dimension and is a far more dangerous threat than any past terrorist movement. Since it is so difficult to combat, it is gradually becoming the predominant mode of warfare (by proxy) in our time. There is some truth in this argument. International state-sponsored terrorism does not offer easy and obvious targets for retaliation, innocents are bound to suffer, and the state which retaliates on a military level will find itself in the role of an aggressor. But the nature of the threat should not be overrated. It will be tolerated only as long as it is not used too frequently and if it does not cause too much damage. If it becomes more than a nuisance, the political calculus changes, and the inhibitions against retaliation no longer function as the public clamour for massive retaliation grows. A process of escalation begins which may result in full-scale military conflict. For this reason, only gross miscalculation will lead the sponsors of state terrorism beyond the point of no return, inviting retaliation which will destroy them. It may happen, but it is unlikely.

10. Terrorism can happen anywhere. This proposition is correct if suitably amended—'except in effective dictator-

ial regimes'. Terrorist operations are frequently carried out by very small groups of people; it is no good enlisting sociology or mass psychology as far as the motives and actions of a few individuals are concerned. For example, the inequities of Sweden's social structure will not explain the murder of Olof Palme.[10] . . .

The Misinterpretation Paradox

There is a paradox involved in the study of terrorism, inasmuch as the basic issues are simple and straightforward. No prolonged training in moral philosophy, psychology or the most modern methods of social research investigation are needed to understand terrorism. Yet at the same time, terrorism is likely to remain the subject of considerable misunderstanding and misinterpretation. Political scientists will find it infertile ground for their hypotheses, and philosophers for their generalizations. The average newspaper reader and television viewer will not easily accept that there is a disproportion between the publicity given to terrorism in the media and its importance in real terms. Those who defend violence (or those who reject it under all circumstances) are bound, sooner or later, to realize that their assumptions are based not on terrorism in general but on one specific kind of terrorism. The difficulty with terrorism is that there is no terrorism *per se*, except perhaps on an abstract level, but different terrorisms. It does not follow that there is no room for objective statements on the subject, that we cannot pass judgement, and should not take action. But each situation has to be viewed in its specific, concrete context, because terrorism is dangerous ground for *simplificateurs* and *généralisateurs*. To approach it, a cool head is probably more essential than any other other intellectual quality.

The importance of terrorism should not be belittled. If the statistics do not bear out the contention that terrorism

10. Swedish prime minister

is steadily rising at an alarming rate, it is also true that there are other weighty arguments concerning the peril of terrorism. The number of victims may be small, but terrorism is designed to undermine government authority, and it may have this effect by showing that democratic governments are unable to respond effectively.

But is it realistic to expect governments which are incapable of stamping out crime, or drug peddling, or illegal immigration, to have full success in the battle against terrorism? Governments cannot protect all of the citizens all of the time against muggers and thieves; likewise, they cannot protect everyone against a terrorist attack. It may well be that, as some argue, terrorism constitutes a potentially serious domestic threat. But much experience has shown that democratic societies seldom take effective measures against *potential* threats. Something akin to a dialectical process seems to be at work: only when the threat becomes clear and present are the authorities and the public sufficiently aroused to agree on the adoption of measures likely to put an end to terrorism, or at least to cause a drastic decline in terrorist activities. A great deal of terrorism could have been prevented during the last two decades [1970s and 1980s] if societies had shown more understanding and governments greater determination. Instead, there was an enormous amount of talk about terrorism and little action. However, if there is a real threat in the years to come it is not so much from the domestic kind of terrorism, which is usually overcome in the end, nor from the possible use of new and more deadly weapons; it is from the danger of escalation—the possibility that terrorism may trigger off a full-scale war.

Terrorism Is a Meaningless Label

JOHN COLLINS

According to author John Collins, the word terrorism *has evolved through various definitions and self-serving connotations depending on the political context of its usage. Collins traces the manipulation of the word* terrorism *through its different meanings in American politics over the past three decades. After the events of September 11, 2001, and in the current war on terrorism, Collins contends, the lack of a clear definition serves governmental purposes. U.S. leaders avoid defining* terrorism *because any definition could be applied to actions America has taken. By refusing to define the term, the United States can use it to condemn acts of political violence against Western or pro-Western states while maintaining an illusion of moral superiority. Collins is assistant professor of global studies at St. Lawrence University, New York.*

A scenario: The U.S. government identifies an Arab as the man responsible for a particular act of political violence, then initiates a retaliatory bombing campaign in the Middle East, generating a wave of patriotic sentiment and xenophobia from Maine to Hawaii. The airwaves are filled with the voices of "terrorism experts" and retired military officers who speak gravely about the need to respond forcefully to "the terrorists." Almost overnight, public opinion polls indicate near-universal support for the notion that "terrorism" is now the country's number one problem.

John Collins, "Terrorism," *Collateral Language: A User's Guide to America's New War*, edited by John Collins and Ross Glover. New York: New York University Press, 2002. Copyright © 2002 by New York University Press. Reproduced by permission.

Strangely, actual definitions of "terrorism" are nowhere to be found. Meanwhile, in the pages of the alternative press, voices of dissent also begin to appear. One article [by author Edward Said] reads as follows:

> Past and future bombing raids aside, the terrorism craze is dangerous because it consolidates the immense, unrestrained pseudopatriotic narcissism we are nourishing. Is there no limit to the folly that convinces large numbers of Americans that it is now unsafe to travel, and at the same time blinds them to all the pain and violence that so many people in Africa, Asia and Latin America must endure simply because we have decided that local oppressors . . . can go on with their killing . . . ? Is there no way to participate in politics beyond the repetition of prefabricated slogans? What happened to the precision, discrimination and critical humanism that we celebrate as the hallmarks of liberal education and the Western heritage?

A "terrorism craze" . . . a rash of "pseudopatriotic narcissism" . . . blindness to the suffering of others . . . public discussion marked by the "repetition of prefabricated slogans"—these are defining characteristics of American society after September 11, 2001. Yet the passage I have just quoted comes not from 2001—nor, for that matter, from the Gulf War of 1991—but rather from an article written by Edward Said in 1986 in the aftermath of the U.S. bombing of Libya. In reviewing future Israeli Prime Minister Benjamin Netanyahu's book *Terrorism: How the West Can Win*, Said argued forcefully that the very notion of "terrorism" needed to be questioned because of its vagueness and because of the way it was being used in the 1980s by policy makers in the United States, Israel, and elsewhere as a label for their political enemies. Looking at the present, post–September 11 situation, one is tempted to conclude that Said's important observations are now as forgotten as the bombing of Libya and the brief period when [Libyan leader] Muammar Qaddafi provided the bridge between [Iranian Imam] Ayatollah Khomeini and [Iraqi leader] Saddam Hussein as the U.S. government's Middle Eastern demon of choice. . . .

U.S. officials actually have rarely provided explicit definitions of "terrorism," relying instead on a vague, even tautological set of descriptions and assumptions that mask the government's own historical role in carrying out, supporting, and provoking political violence. Thus we have a situation in which Americans are being asked to support an open-ended war not against a clearly defined "enemy," but rather against an ideological concept whose definition is assumed rather than offered.

In this light, I argue that the obvious and important question now being asked by critically minded citizens (What, exactly, is "terrorism"?) needs to be modified to take into account the process through which the concept of "terrorism" was *made understandable* to Americans. The question then becomes, What is "terrorism" such that we can declare war on it?

The Historical Invention of "Terrorism"

In its earliest usage, the concept of "terrorism" surfaced in the aftermath of the French revolution, when the nation's new leaders employed a "reign of terror" to eliminate their political enemies and consolidate their hold on power. We also know that nineteenth-century Russian revolutionaries were labeled "terrorists" because they used violence to pursue their political ends. As late as 1965, the word "terrorism" had not entered into popular usage in the United States. Scarcely a decade later, however, the term had acquired a very specific set of meanings, and ordinary citizens understood political leaders who invoked "terrorism" as a "threat." How did this change happen? . . .

The government's steadily increasing preoccupation with "terrorism" had a direct impact on the research agendas of social scientists working in international relations, security studies, and other policy-related fields. By the mid-1970s, "terrorism" was fast becoming a cottage industry in academia; more than a dozen books were published on the subject in 1975 alone. . . .

It is impossible to understand "terrorism" without understanding the close relationship between the government and the academy. When this relationship is expanded to include private think tanks, corporations, the media, and the military, we begin to see the full complexity of the institutional web in which "terrorism experts" have operated since the 1970s. . . .

The ability of the same "experts" to appear in multiple institutions ensures not only that their personal views will be widely disseminated, but also that the range of available opinion on "terrorism" will be narrow, for virtually all those recognized as "experts" share a common set of assumptions. In fact, the dominant understanding of what constitutes "terrorism" has changed little in recent decades, even though a variety of individuals and groups have occupied the role of "terrorist." In the eyes of the "experts" who provided the initial framing of the issue in the 1970s, "terrorism" represented a fundamental challenge to the authority of the state. Under the dominant definition, however, "terrorism" could only be directed against particular kinds of states, namely, Western or pro-Western states such as the United States and other nations (such as England, West Germany, or Israel) that belonged to the anti-Soviet bloc. In other words, out of all the political violence in the world, the damning label of "terrorism" was applied only to violence that came from the Left or (less frequently and in the European context) from the far Right. Political violence carried out by or with the support of the United States and its allies, by contrast, was known by a host of less pejorative terms: counterinsurgency, counterterrorism, low-intensity conflict, self-defense, and war. . . .

"Terrorism" and Political Violence

As I have already suggested, "terrorism" is nothing more than a name given to a small subset of actions within the much larger category of political violence. What distinguishes "terrorism" from other acts of political violence, of course, depends on who is doing the defining (or non-defining, as we will see below). From the perspective of analysts who are concerned with defending U.S. economic and military supremacy, the safest definition, now as in the 1970s, is that "terrorism" involves organized opposition to the policies of the United States or its allies. By this definition, it is literally impossible for the U.S. government to commit or support acts of "terrorism." In this case, using the language of "terrorism"—and, at the extreme, declaring war on it—is one way for U.S. officials and supporters of U.S. policies to downplay the immense human suffering that continues to occur as a result of those policies.

Yet the evidence of this suffering is all around us, and this is where other existing definitions of "terrorism" run into the problem of double standards. Each possible definition has its referents in specific U.S. actions. Violence used to achieve political ends? The Vietnam War (or any other war). Violence perpetrated by nonstate actors against a sovereign state? The Nicaraguan *contras*. Violence committed by a nondemocratic government against its own population? The repression carried out by U.S.-trained dictators in Latin America. Violence targeting innocent civilians? The U.S. bombing of water-treatment facilities in Iraq during the Gulf War. Violence designed to create panic among a population and put pressure on their government? The bombing of Hiroshima and Nagasaki.

Evading Definitions

The point here is that *any* explicit definition of "terrorism" could be used to identify and condemn the actions of the United States and many of its allies. Maintaining the illusion of U.S. blamelessness, therefore, *requires that "terrorism" not be defined at all.* Consequently, instead of definitions we find tautological evasions. For example, when Secretary of State George Shultz gave a speech on "terrorism" to the Park Avenue Synagogue in New York in 1984, he offered a curious observation: "Terrorism is a modern barbarism that we call terrorism." Seventeen years later, when George W. Bush addressed the U.S. Congress to declare his war on "terrorism," he could do no better, speaking vaguely of "terrorists" as "enemies of freedom." Any sense of the specificity of "terrorism"—that is, anything that might distinguish "terrorism" as a particular form of political violence—was lost when the president argued that the September 11 attacks were "an act of war" and that the perpetrators "follow in the path of fascism, Nazism and totalitarianism." A key statement by Secretary of Defense Donald Rumsfeld, published in the *New York Times* shortly before the United States began bombing Afghanistan [in October 2001], contained nothing resembling a definition; the war, Rumsfeld wrote, was simply against "terrorism's attack on our way of life."

Perhaps the most telling moment in the current situation, however, occurred during the United Nations General Assembly's extraordinary weeklong (October 1–5, 2001) "Debate on measures to eliminate international terrorism." Representatives of one hundred seventy nations rose to speak on the issue, and while all condemned the attacks of September 11, many also made careful reference to the double standards and blind spots inherent in the implicit, dominant definition of "terrorism.". . .

UK representative Sir Peter Greenstock . . . offered token recognition of . . . Third World critiques, only to silence them with his own redundancy: "Increasingly, questions are being raised about the problem of the definition of a terrorist. Let us be wise and focused about this: *terrorism is terrorism.* . . . There is common ground amongst all of us on what constitutes terrorism. What looks, smells and kills like terrorism is terrorism" (emphasis added).

It should be noted that Greenstock is considerably less skilled in the art of nondefinition than many of his American and Israeli counterparts, for his remarks ironically give legitimacy to the perspectives of non-Western communities whose victimization has never been recognized in the dominant language of "terrorism." Palestinians, after all, know better than anyone that military occupation "looks, smells and kills like terrorism." Afghans, Iraqis, and Panamanians could say the same thing about aerial bombardment; Salvadorans and Guatemalans could testify to the "terrorism" of military death squads; Angolans, Cambodians, and Mozambicans are experts on the long-term terrorizing effects of land mines; Vietnamese and Lebanese have lived the horrible reality of chemical warfare in the form of napalm and phosphorous shells; and the list goes on. Taking the argument further, one could say that the global economy itself, organized and governed primarily according to the needs of U.S.-based transnational corporations, is the ultimate producer of "terror" for populations across the globe. What, after all, is more "terrifying" than systematic, widespread hunger and hopelessness? A Brazilian anarchist group perhaps had this point in mind when it circulated the following statement after the September 11 attacks:

> 35,615 children died out of starvation on September 11, 2001
> victims: 35,615 children (source: FAO)
> where: poor countries
> special tv programs: none
> newspaper articles: none
> messages from the president: none
> solidarity acts: none
> minutes of silence: none
> victims mournings: none
> organized forums: none
> pope messages: none
> stock exchanges: didn't care
> euro: kept its way
> alert level: zero
> army mobilization: none
> conspiracy theories: none
> main suspects: rich countries

This is why tautology is safer than any sort of qualitative description. U.S. officials, having learned this lesson long ago, know that the best way to avoid the issue altogether is to locate "terrorism" squarely in the individuals upon whom public anger is periodically focused: [Yasir] Arafat, Khomeini, Saddam, [Osama] bin Laden.

We are left, then, with a remarkable example of circular logic, with the political equivalent of a cat endlessly chasing its tail. The operative, unstated definition of "terrorism" at work in the "war on terrorism" runs roughly as follows: *"Terrorism" is what "terrorists" do. And who are the "terrorists"? Well, we know who they are, because we have already identified them—they are the ones who commit "terrorism."*

Most Textbooks Fail to Correctly Define Terrorism

STANLEY MICHALAK

In the following selection, Stanley Michalak argues that college textbooks do a poor job of defining terrorism. For example, he contends that the textbooks define terrorism so broadly as to include any use of force, suggesting that even legitimate military responses to terrorist attacks are themselves terrorism. The books also resort to moral equivalency by stating the often-repeated cliché that "one person's terrorist is another person's freedom fighter." Contrary to the intellectually questionable claims of these textbooks, he insists, terrorism is easily defined as "random and horrific acts of violence against unsuspecting and innocent non-combatants." Michalak is a professor of government at Franklin and Marshall College.

W hen the shock of 9/11 was drawing down, I decided to peruse the international relations textbooks on my home and office shelves. "What would students learn," I asked, "if they consulted any of these texts in order to make sense out of the events that so shocked the nation?" What I found in reading these works was in most cases simply appalling—and I consulted not one or two, but ten in all—ten textbooks published by such major houses as Addison-Wesley, Dushkin/McGraw Hill, Harcourt Brace,

Stanley Michalak, "Are College Textbooks Miseducating Students About Terrorism?" http://hnn.us, November 25, 2002. Copyright © 2002 by the History News Network. Reproduced by permission.

Longman, McGraw Hill, Prentice Hall, Simon and Schuster, and W.W. Norton (and listed at the end of this essay). What I found were sloppy definitions, specious moral equivalencies, the uncritical perpetuation of myths about terrorism, descriptive unanalytical filler, superficiality, and banality.

What is terrorism? On this rather simple question, no consensus exists among these texts. Some define terrorism so broadly as to make it indistinguishable from any use of force. For example, does it serve any purpose to define terrorism as "seeking to further political objectives through the threat or use of violence usually in opposition to state governments?" (Kegley and Wittkopf, p. 222) or "the use of violence to achieve a political objective" (Papp, p. 127). What would not be considered terrorism under these definitions? Does it make sense to throw coercive diplomacy and conventional war into the same bucket as terrorism?

Sure it does, if one is seeking to create moral equivalencies between terrorists and their victims. As one author writes, ". . . defining terrorism is a difficult task." "Indeed," the author continues, "several countries throughout the world consider the United States, several Western European states, and Israel as undertaking terrorist actions" (Papp, p. 14).

False Equations of Moral Equivalency

While all of the texts make a stab at defining terrorism, we quickly learn from the vast majority of them that terrorism lies largely in the eyes of the beholder. Almost all, in fact, trot out uncritically the cliche that one "person's" terrorist is another "person's" freedom fighter. One text makes this point four times in about eight pages devoted to the subject. Even a six-line description of the Terrorism Research Center's website contains a warning to students that in looking at "terrorist profiles and the Definition of Terrorism controversy, keep in mind that one group's 'freedom fighters' may be another group's 'terrorists'" (Kegley and Wittkopf, p. 241).

Four warnings in eight pages.

If students learn only one thing from most of these texts it is this: While no one really knows what terrorism is, whatever it is, we are one, as well. Consider the following examples: "To a great extent, whether an organization is defined as a terrorist group or not depends on one's perspective. When seen from an American perspective, the 'Indians' of the Boston Tea Party were American nationalists making a political point: when seen from a British perspective, they were terrorists destroying property and endangering life" (Papp, p. 127).

"Pressure to respond to [random acts of terrorism] is very strong because people worry disproportionately about terrorism, even though it kills a relatively small number of people. Despite better devices for protection, committed individuals or groups of terrorists are difficult to deter. As the well-known phrase puts it, one person's terrorists is another person's freedom fighter" (Mingst, p. 179).

"It is easy to condemn such [terrorist] activities when they are conducted by countries or groups with which you disapprove. What about assassination and other such actions by a country with which you may have sympathy? . . . Those who question the legitimacy of such acts [Reagan's strike against Qaddafi and Clinton's strikes in Somalia and Afghanistan] argue that what constitutes terrorism is often in the eye of the beholder and, in this case, killing civilians with a bomb dropped on a building by a warplane is no different than (sic) killing civilians by planting a bomb in a building" (Rourke, pp. 346–47).

As the last quotation indicates, some authors hedge their equations of moral equivalency in a veil of specious objectivity through attributions to often unnamed "some" or "observers." Consider the following from the author last quoted: "It should be noted that in the view of some, the way that the United States and some other militarily powerful countries define terrorism is self-serving" (Rourke, p. 347). And who are the "some"? Well, in this case, one of the "somes" is none other than Osama bin Laden. According to the author, "Osama bin Laden, who allegedly masterminded the attacks on the US embassy in Kenya and Tanzania in 1988, charges that, 'American history does not distinguish between civilians and military, and not even women and children. [Americans] are the ones who used the [atomic] bombs against the Japanese'" (Rourke, p. 347).

While it's one thing to point out that people use the term terrorist in self-serving and indiscriminate ways, it's quite another to throw up one's hands at defining what terrorism is. Clearly, we know what contemporary terrorism is: it is a strategy that explicitly targets innocent civilians. Thus, America's retaliation against Qaddafi for the Berlin disco bombing was not an act of terrorism, as terrifying as that response may have been and as tragic as the civilian deaths may have been. The target in those attacks was not innocent civilians but the perpetuator and root of the terrorist campaign.

To label as "terrorist" any violent action that results in civilian deaths makes any effort to classify the uses of force impossible. Neither ends nor consequences but means defines terrorism. Terrorism used in a good cause is terrorism, nonetheless, and even the best of good causes can never make terrorism good or moral as Michael Walzer pointed out in his book *Just and Unjust Wars* over twenty years ago. Using random and horrific acts of violence against unsuspecting and innocent non-combatants is terrorism, and moral people will condemn such acts no matter who undertakes them.

Myths and Lies Surrounding Terrorism

Rather than engaging in what Charles Hyneman once termed, "the rigorous examination of ideas," too many of these political scientists merely pass on and legitimize egregiously shallow and uncritical thinking. For example, one of the most simplistic myths perpetuated by almost all of these texts is the portrayal of terrorists as powerless, despair-driven people—"the international homeless," as one set of authors put it. Terrorism, we are told, is "usually used by the powerless against the powerful" (Mingst, p. 178); it is "the strategy of the weak for weakening the strong" (Roskin and Berry, p. 4). "Terrorist groups," according to another text, "seek the political freedom, privilege, and property they think persecution has denied them" (Kegley and Wittkopf, p. 222). Somewhat strangely, the authors of this last assertion devote their first case study to "international organized crime," which they claim is "one increasingly active category of terrorist groups" (p. 222).

Obviously, most terrorists do not have the military capabilities of the parties against whom they wage war; however, military asymmetry by itself does not mean that terrorist groups are powerless, weak, or even poor. Hizbollah, Hamas, and Al Qaeda [Islamic terrorist groups]—even when these books were written—could not be considered groups comprised of the uneducated, "great unwashed." Al Qaeda is as well financed as any terrorist organization can be, and its leaders and many of its minions are or have been well educated. Moreover, to say that members of terrorist organizations are powerless implicitly accepts and legitimizes their rejection of normal and peaceful measures for settling differences. Hamas and Hizbollah do not want a settlement with Israel; they want Israelis expunged from the Middle East. Timothy McVeigh was not seeking to argue his case in the American political arena; he wanted to destroy that very arena.

But the more important myth lies on the other side of the equation—that the targets of terrorism are "the powerful." As Walter Laqueur pointed out almost thirty years ago, terrorism rarely occurs in powerful countries such as Iraq, Syria, North Korea, the Soviet Union, Mao's China, Iran, Saudi Arabia, or even in Afghanistan during the reign of the Taliban. Since the end of the Second World War, the targets of terrorism have been concentrated in permissive democracies such as the United States, Great Britain, and the

Western European social democracies or soft authoritarian regimes such as Egypt and Algeria. Truly powerful and totalitarian regimes never have a problem with terrorists. . . .

Superficialities in Contemporary Scholarship

From reading these texts, it is not even clear whether terrorism is a significant problem, although most do predict its persistence and, in several cases, authors dangle truly apocalyptic scenarios in which we, in the democracies, stand helpless and, presumably, hopeless. However, consider the following two assessments—drawn from the same database and scholarly literature: "Given the nature of the problem and the draconian methods that would probably be required to eliminate it, it is likely that terrorism will be with the international community for the foreseeable future" (Papp, p. 29).

"Terrorism, despite occasional outbursts, is in decline. The same forces that are reshaping international relations in other areas are also reducing terrorist violence. The end of the Cold War brought about major power cooperation. This removed the target for many ideological terrorists groups. . . . In addition, the worldwide rise of democracy has reduced domestic terrorism directed against repressive regimes" (Roskin and Berry, 1999 ed., p. 252). . . .

While most of the works surveyed do cite solid scholarly works on terrorism in their bibliographies, very little of the knowledge in those books makes its way into their discussions of the subject! Many of the myths about terrorism that Walter Laqueur debunked over twenty-five years ago in his groundbreaking book *Terrorism* appear in far too many of these texts.

Sadly, discussions of terrorism in most of today's textbooks amount to melodramatic or sensational introductions, portraits of different kinds of terrorists, descriptive case studies, and superficial assessments about the future— all low-level, unanalytical, and simplistic stuff. What is also dismaying about these texts is what they reveal about the state of the discipline. In fact, reading most of these texts quickly leads one to wonder what the "higher" in higher education means at the nation's colleges and universities.

Texts Reviewed

Caldwell, Dan, *World Politics and You* (Upper Saddle River, NJ: Prentice Hall, 2000). Subject not covered.

Duncan, W. Raymond, Barbara Jancar-Webster, and Bob Switky, *World Politics in the 21st Century* (New York: Addison-Wesley/Longman Inc., 2002).

Kegley, Jr., Charles and Eugene R. Wittkopf, *World Politics: Trend and Transformation* (Bedford: St. Martins, 2001).

Mingst, Karen, *Essentials of International Relations* (New York: W.W. Norton & Company, 2001, second edition).

Papp, Daniel S., *Contemporary International Relations: Frameworks for Understanding* (New York: Longman, 2002, sixth edition).

Pearson, Fredric S. and J. Martin Rochester, *International Relations: The Global Condition in the Twenty-First Century* (New York: McGraw Hill, 1997, fourth edition).

Roskin, Michael G. and Nicholas O. Berry, *IR: The New World of International Relations* (Upper Saddle River, NJ: Prentice-Hall, 1999, fourth edition).

Roskin, Michael G. and Nicholas O. Berry, *IR: The New World of International Relations* (Upper Saddle River, NJ: Prentice-Hall, 2002, fifth edition).

Rourke, John T., *International Politics on the World Stage* (Dushkin/McGraw-Hill, 1999, seventh edition).

Ziegler, David, *War, Peace, and International Politics* (New York: Addison, Wesley, Longman, 2000).

50 B.C.–A.D. 41

Julius Caesar is the first in a series of Roman emperors who quash opposition with terror tactics, including torture and the abduction of political prisoners.

A.D. 50

In ancient Rome, Jewish insurgent terrorists known as Sicarii use concealed daggers to stab their victims at open-air festivals.

1000–1250

Trained assassins, followers of Ismaili extremist Hassan-i-Sabbah, murder enemies of their leader for a reward of eternal paradise.

1785

In June pirates from North Africa's Barbary Coast take twenty-one sailors hostage and demand a ransom from the U.S. government for their release. In the next thirty years, more than seven hundred American sailors from thirty-five different ships are taken hostage.

1793

Between September 5, 1793, and July 27, 1794, during the French Reign of Terror, more than sixteen thousand people are publicly executed by guillotine. For the first time the label *terrorism* is used.

1866

The Ku Klux Klan begins terrorizing African Americans in the South.

1920

On September 16, thirty-five people die when a dynamite bomb explodes on Wall Street in New York City. The bombing, blamed on Communists but detonated from the horse-drawn wagon of a known anarchist named Mario Buda, launches an era of anti-Communist sentiment known as the Red Scare.

1941–1945

Six million Jews die at the hands of Nazi terrorists during World War II.

1946

On July 22, the Jewish extremist group Irgun bombs the King David Hotel in Palestine. Ninety-one people are killed and forty-five are injured.

1954

On June 27, democratically elected president Jacobo Arbenz Guzmán of Guatemala is overthrown by a coup orchestrated by the U.S. Central Intelligence Agency (CIA). On July 8, military dictator Carlos Castillo Armas takes control.

1961

The first skyjacking of a U.S. aircraft occurs on May 1 when Antulio Ramirez Ortiz hijacks a National Airlines plane en route from Key West, Florida, to Havana, Cuba.

1963

On September 15, Ku Klux Klansman Robert Chambliss, assisted by other Klansmen, bombs the Sixteenth Street Baptist Church in Birmingham, Alabama, killing four African American girls.

1972

On July 21, a day known as Bloody Friday, an Irish Republican Army (IRA) bomb explodes in Belfast, Northern Ireland, killing eleven people and injuring 130. On September 5, at the summer Olympics in Munich, West Germany, eight Palestinian members of the Black September terrorist group seize eleven Israeli athletes. Nine of the hostages are killed.

1973

On September 11, in a military coup in Chile, Augusto Pinochet takes power from democratically elected president Salvador Allende. Thousands of Pinochet's enemies are tortured and killed, said to have "disappeared."

1979

On November 4, in Tehran, Iran, a group of radicals seize the U.S. embassy and take sixty-six people hostage. Fifty-three of them are held until January 20, 1981. On November 20, at the Grand Mosque in Mecca, Saudi Arabia, as many as two hundred Islamic terrorists take hundreds of pilgrims hostage, and when the siege ends more than 250 people are dead.

1980

On December 2, in an act of state-sponsored terrorism, a military death squad in San Salvador, El Salvador, kidnaps, rapes, and executes three American nuns and a missionary. In Nicaragua, contra terrorists gain training and funds. Thousands of Nicaraguan civilians die at the hands of the contras.

1983

In April the terrorist group Islamic Jihad explodes a suicide truck bomb at the U.S. embassy in Beirut, Lebanon. Sixty-three people are killed and 120 injured. In October, Islamic Jihad launches truck bomb attacks on American and French military compounds, killing 242 American and 58 French troops.

1985

In February Drug Enforcement Administration official Enrique Salazar and his pilot are kidnapped, tortured, and killed by narcoterrorist Rafael Quintero. On December 27, Islamic terrorists hurl grenades and fire machine guns at the ticket counters of El Al and TWA airlines in Fiumicino International Airport in Rome. Sixteen people die and eighty are injured.

1988

On December 21, 270 people die when two Libyan terrorists blow up Pan Am Flight 103 over Lockerbie, Scotland.

1993

On February 26, Islamic extremists bomb the World Trade Center in New York City. Six people are killed and more than a thousand are injured.

1994

On February 25, Jewish right-wing extremist and U.S. citizen Dr. Baruch Goldstein fires an assault rifle on Muslim worshippers attending Friday prayers at a mosque in Hebron, West Bank. Twenty-nine people die and 150 are injured.

1995

On March 20, in an act of domestic terrorism, members of the Aum Shinrikyo millennium cult release toxic sarin gas into the crowded Tokyo subway system. Twelve people die and more than fifty-seven hundred people are injured. On April 19, right-wing extremist Timothy McVeigh uses a rented truck filled with explosives to destroy the Alfred P. Murrah Federal Building in Oklahoma City, killing 168 people.

1996

On June 15, the IRA detonates a truck bomb at a shopping center, in Manchester, England, wounding 206 people. On June 25, a truck bomb explodes outside Khobar Towers, a U.S. military housing facility in Dhahran, Saudi Arabia. Nineteen people are killed and 515 are injured.

1998

On August 7, the U.S. embassies in Nairobi, Kenya, and Dar es Salaam, Tanzania, are struck by suicide truck bomb attacks. Two hundred thirteen people in Nairobi and twelve in Dar es Salaam are killed; five thousand people are injured. The attacks are linked to al Qaeda and Osama bin Laden.

2000

On October 12, seventeen sailors from the USS *Cole* die in Yemen when a small dinghy packed with explosives attacks the destroyer. The attack is linked to al Qaeda and Osama bin Laden.

2001

On September 11, Islamic terrorists hijack four airplanes and turn them into flying bombs. Two destroy the World Trade Center towers, one hits the Pentagon, and another lands in a Pennsylvania field. The death toll reaches 2,752 people. Al Qaeda terrorists under the instruction of Osama bin Laden are held responsible.

2004

In May, American businessman Nicholas Berg is decapitated in Iraq by Islamic terrorists. Berg's killers are presumed to have links with al Qaeda. On September 1, multinational terrorists (mainly Chechen and Ingush) laid siege to a primary school in Beslan, Russia. More than 350 people were killed, including 156 children, and 434 were wounded.

Organizations to Contact

The editors have compiled the following list of organizations concerned with the topics contained in this book. The descriptions are derived from materials provided by the organizations. All have publications or information available for interested readers. The list was compiled on the date of publication of the present volume; the information provided here may change. Be aware that many organizations take several weeks or longer to respond to inquiries, so allow as much time as possible.

American Civil Liberties Union (ACLU)
125 Broad St., 18th Fl., New York, NY 10004-2400
(212) 549-2500
e-mail: aclu@aclu.org • Web site: www.aclu.org

The American Civil Liberties Union is a national organization that works to defend Americans' civil rights. The ACLU argues that measures to protect national security in the wake of terrorist attacks should not compromise civil liberties. Its publications include *Civil Liberties After 9-11: The ACLU Defends Freedom* and *National ID Cards: 5 Reasons Why They Should Be Rejected.*

Anti-Defamation League (ADL)
823 United Nations Plaza, New York, NY 10017
(212) 885-7700 • fax: (212) 867-0779
Web site: www.adl.org

The Anti-Defamation League is a human relations organization that fights all forms of prejudice and bigotry. The Web site features extensive information on Israel, the Middle East, and terrorism, including information on terrorist groups and articles such as "Terrorism and Moral Clarity" and "Give Security Agencies More Room to Fight Terrorism." The ADL also publishes the bimonthly online newsletter *Frontline.*

Brookings Institution
1775 Massachusetts Ave. NW, Washington, DC 20036
(202) 797-6000 • fax: (202) 797-6004
e-mail: brookinfo@brook.edu • Web site: www.brook.edu

The Brookings Institution conducts foreign policy research and analyzes global events and their impact on the United States. The institution publishes the *Brookings Review* quarterly, along with numerous papers and books on foreign policy. Publications related to terrorism include *Nasty, Brutish and Long: America's War on Terrorism* and *Protecting the American Homeland: One Year On.*

Center for Strategic and International Studies (CSIS)
1800 K St. NW, Washington, DC 20006
(202) 887-0200 • fax: (202) 775-3199
Web site: www.csis.org

CSIS is a public policy research institution that focuses on America's economic policy, national security, and foreign and domestic policy. The center analyzes global crises and suggests U.S. military policies. Its publications include the journal *Washington Quarterly* and the studies *Protecting Against the Spread of Nuclear, Biological, and Chemical Weapons* and *Cyberthreats, Information Warfare, and Critical Infrastructure Protection: Defending the U.S. Homeland.*

Council on American-Islamic Relations (CAIR)
453 New Jersey Ave. SE, Washington, DC 20003
(202) 488-8787 • fax: (202) 488-0833
e-mail: cair@cair-net.org • Web site: www.cair-net.org

CAIR is a nonprofit organization that challenges stereotypes of Islam and Muslims and offers an Islamic perspective on public policy issues. Its publications include action alerts, news briefs, and the quarterly newsletter *Faith in Action.* The CAIR Web site features statements condemning both the September 11, 2001, terrorist attacks and subsequent discrimination against Muslims.

Council on Foreign Relations
58 E. Sixty-eighth St., New York, NY 10021
(212) 434-9400 • fax: (212) 434-9800
e-mail: communications@cfr.org • Web site: www.cfr.org

The council researches the international aspects of American economic and social policies. Its journal *Foreign Affairs*, published five times a year, provides analysis on global conflicts. Publications relating to terrorism include the anthology *The War on Terror*, the report *Threats to Democracy: Prevention and Response*, and various articles.

Global Exchange
2017 Mission, #303, San Francisco, CA 94110
(415) 255-7296 • fax: (415) 255-7498
Web site: www.globalexchange.org

Global Exchange is a human rights organization that aims to expose economic and political injustice. It believes the best solution to such injustices is education, activism, and a noninterventionist U.S. foreign policy. Global Exchange opposes military retaliation in response to terrorist attacks. Books on terrorism are available for purchase on its Web site, and the organization also publishes a quarterly newsletter.

Heritage Foundation
214 Massachusetts Ave. NE, Washington, DC 20002-4999
(800) 544-4843 • (202) 546-4400 • fax: (202) 544-6979
e-mail: pubs@heritage.org • Web site: www.heritage.org

The Heritage Foundation is a public policy research institute that supports limited government and the free-market system. The foundation publishes the quarterly journal *Policy Review*, along with papers, books, and monographs. Heritage publications about the war on terrorism include *The Vital Role of Alliances in the Global War on Terrorism* and *Presidential Authority in the War on Terrorism: Iraq and Beyond.*

International Policy Institute for Counter-Terrorism (ICT)
PO Box 167, Herzlia, 46150, Israel
972-9-9527277 • fax: 972-9-9513073
e-mail: info@ict.org.il • Web site: www.ict.org.il

ICT is a research institute that develops public policy solutions to international terrorism. Its Web site is a comprehensive resource on terrorism and counterterrorism, including an extensive database on terrorist organizations. Numerous articles on terrorism are published on the Web site, including "The Continuing Al-Qaeda Threat" and "The Changing Threat of International Terrorism."

Middle East Research and Information Project (MERIP)
1500 Massachusetts Ave. NW, Suite 119, Washington, DC 20005
(202) 223-3677 • fax: (202) 223-3604
e-mail: ctoensing@merip.org • Web site: www.merip.org

MERIP is a nonprofit organization that has no ties to any religious, political, or educational organization. The project believes that stereotypes and misconceptions have kept the United States and Europe from fully understanding the Middle East. MERIP aims to end this misunderstanding by addressing a wide range of political, cultural, and social issues and by publishing writings by authors from the Middle East. MERIP publishes the quarterly magazine *Middle East Report*, op-ed pieces, and *Middle East Report Online*, which includes Web-only analysis and commentary.

National Memorial Institute for the Prevention of Terrorism (MIPT)
PO Box 889, Oklahoma City, Oklahoma 73101
(405) 232-5121 • fax: (405) 232-5132
e-mail: research@mipt.org • Web site: www.mipt.org

MIPT is a nonprofit organization that conducts research into counterterrorism strategies and the effects of terrorism and hosts conferences of terrorism experts. Part of the MIPT mission is to draw attention to the contributions of first responders on the scene of terrorist attacks.

U.S. Department of State Counterterrorism Office
Office of the Coordinator for Counterterrorism
Office of Public Affairs, Room 2509, U.S. Department of State, 2201 C St. NW, Washington, DC 20520
(202) 647-4000
e-mail: http://contact-us.state.gov

The U.S. Department of State is a federal agency that advises the president on foreign policy matters. The Office of Counterterrorism publishes the annual report *Patterns of Global Terrorism*, a list of the United States' most wanted terrorists, and numerous fact sheets and press releases on the war on terrorism.

Washington Institute for Near East Policy
1828 L St. NW, Suite 1050, Washington, DC 20036
(202) 452-0650 • fax: (202) 223-5364
e-mail: info@washingtoninstitute.org
Web site: www.washingtoninstitute.org

The institute is an independent organization that researches and analyzes Middle Eastern issues and U.S. policy in the region. Its Web site features several publications on terrorism, including the anthology *America and the Middle East: Expanding Threat, Broadening Response*, and several PolicyWatches, among them "Patterns of Terrorism 2002."

Web Sites

America Responds
Web site: www.pbs.org/americaresponds/educators.html

In the days following the September 11 attack on America, the Public Broadcasting Service compiled a collection of useful and pertinent resources on the subject of terrorism. The site has been maintained and expanded to include information on emergency preparedness, cultural conflicts, and geographical and historical facts.

Terrorism Research Center
Web site: www.terrorism.com

The goal of the Terrorism Research Center is to inform the public about terrorism and information warfare. The Web site features profiles of terrorist organizations, essays and analysis, and links to other terrorism-related documents and resources.

For Further Research

Yonah Alexander, *Control of Terrorism: International Documents*. New York: Crane Russak, 1979.

Sean Anderson, *Historical Dictionary of Terrorism*. 2nd ed. Historical Dictionaries of Religions, Philosophies, and Movements, no. 4. Lanham, MD: Scarecrow Press, 2002.

Patricia Baird-Windle, *Targets of Hatred: Anti-Abortion Terrorism*. New York: Palgrave, 2001.

Benjamin R. Barber, *Fear's Empire: War, Terrorism, and Democracy*. New York: W.W. Norton, 2003.

Caleb Carr, *The Lessons of Terror: A History of Warfare Against Civilians: Why It Has Always Failed and Why It Will Fail Again*. New York: Random House, 2002.

Noam Chomsky, *9-11*. New York: Seven Stories Press, 2001.

John Collins and Ross Glover, eds., *Collateral Language: A User's Guide to America's New War*. New York: New York University Press, 2002.

John Dinges, *The Condor Years: How Pinochet and His Allies Brought Terrorism to Three Continents*. New York: New Press, 2004.

Richard Falk, *The Great Terror War*. New York: Olive Branch Press, 2003.

John George and Laird Wilcox, *American Extremists: Militias, Supremacists, Klansmen, Communists, and Others*. Amherst, NY: Prometheus, 1996.

Bill Gertz, *Breakdown: How America's Intelligence Failures Led to September 11*. Washington, DC: Regnery, 2002.

Philip Heymann, *Terrorism and America: A Commonsense Strategy for a Democratic Society*. Cambridge, MA: MIT Press, 1998.

Bruce Hoffman, *Inside Terrorism*. New York: Columbia University Press, 1998.

Chalmers Johnson, *Blowback: The Costs and Consequences of American Empire*. New York: Metropolitan Books, 2004.

Walter Laqueur, *The Age of Terrorism*. New York: Little, Brown, 1987.

————, *No End to War: Terrorism in the Twenty-first Century*. New York: Continuum, 2003.

Dennis Piszkiewicz, *Terrorism's War with America*. Westport, CT: Praeger, 2003.

Tom Pyszczynski, with Sheldon Solomon and Jeff Greenberg, *In the Wake of 9/11: The Psychology of Terror*. Washington, DC: American Psychological Association, 2003.

Arundhati Roy, *War Talk*. Cambridge: South End Press, 2003.

Phil Scraton, ed., *Beyond September 11: An Anthology of Dissent*. Sterling, VA: Pluto, 2002.

Jeffrey D. Simon, *The Terrorist Trap*. Bloomington: Indiana University Press, 2001.

Andrew Sinclair, *An Anatomy of Terror: A History of Terrorism*. London: Macmillan, 2003.

Mary Smyth and Marie-Therese Fay, eds., *Personal Accounts from Northern Ireland's Troubles: Public Conflict, Private Loss*. Sterling, VA: Pluto, 2000.

Terry Waite, *Taken on Trust*. New York: Harcourt, 1993.

Frederic Wakeman Jr., *The Shanghai Badlands: Wartime Terrorism and Urban Crime.* New York: Cambridge University Press, 1996.

Michael Walzer, *Just and Unjust Wars.* New York: BasicBooks, 1977.

Paul L. Williams, *Al Qaeda: Brotherhood of Terror.* Parsippany, NJ: Alpha, 2002.

Index